D0778465

MAR 15 2001

*Words & Wisdom of the
Appliance Doctor*

Words & Wisdom of the
APPLIANCE DOCTOR

By Joe Gagnon

Sleeping Bear Press

Sleeping Bear Press
310 North Main Street
P.O. Box 20
Chelsea, MI 48118
www.sleepingbearpress.com

Printed and bound in the United States.

10 9 8 7 6 5 4 3 2 1

Library of Congress Cataloging-in-Publication Data on file
ISBN: 1-886947-67-8

This book is dedicated to my sixth child,
Hollie, whom I cherish.

Joe Gagnon

❧

Thanks to Glenn Haege of WXYT Radio and
his publishing company, Master Handyman Press,
for allowing me to use a few words from my first
book, *First Aid on Appliances.*

Table of Contents

Foreword

In 1999, in my first year in office, Joe Gagnon invited me to be a guest on his Appliance Doctor radio show. On this particular day, we were taping the show from the floor of the North American International Auto Show in Detroit's Cobo Hall. The radio station's booth, perched high above the convention's main floor was sandwiched on a thin stretch of carpeted walkway between a temporary auditorium and a collection of vintage cars. Not only were we difficult to find in this sea of autos and auto-philes, but in the heart of Motor City, surrounded by the hottest new wheels in the world, the state's Attorney General was obviously one of the day's "B-list" attractions. Clearly, I was underestimating Joe Gagnon's star power.

During an on-air break, a young man emerged from the crowd, stepped up to the booth and pulled a small, hand-held tape recorder from the pocket of his coat. He held it across the shallow desk, popped it on near Joe's ear, and asked earnestly, "So Doc, what do you think?"

Joe listened for a moment, stopped the tape, rewound it and then, over the din of the convention below us, he declared it a dying dryer motor. "Oh yeah," he said, "dryer's on the fritz, huh? Sounds like you need a new..." And he rattled off a list of replacement parts just as the radio show's producer whispered in my ear that we were live again in 5...4...3...2...

I heard that tape that day, too. I held it up to my ear just like Joe did and I'm sure that the "whrrr, whrrr, kchunk" I heard must have been something altogether different than the immediately recognizable, diagnosable and repairable clothes dryer that Joe heard.

I don't know for sure, but I don't think that young man came to Cobo Hall that day to ogle cars or to kick tires. I think he came all the way downtown, through the traffic, through the crowd, up the stairs, and all the way to the back of the hall between the old cars and the new auditorium, just to have the Appliance Doctor listen to his sick machine.

That's why Joe's so special. Oh sure, he can recommend a quality oven or troubleshoot a sputtering furnace, but it's his commitment to really listening to consumers and their concerns that has made him such a treasure. In my own office, we send people Joe's way all the time. In fact, over the years, thousands of Michiganians have turned to Joe for his unique blend of suggestions, stories and advice—I have no doubt that his words will fix what ails your appliances, too.

And believe me, someday, when you find yourself down on your knees catching the idiosyncrasies of your clothes dryer on tape, you'll be glad you own this book and that Joe's only a phone call away.

Joe Gagnon, the Appliance Doctor, my hero.

—Jennifer M. Granholm,
Michigan State Attorney General

The Appliance Doctor

Just Who am I to Tell You What to Do, Anyway?

Upfront and Personal

More than 30 years ago, I was hired by a manufacturer to teach the appliance service industry to others. I met a lot of good people along the way, people with good and ethical business practices. But I also met crooks that made me feel ashamed to be associated with in the same industry. It didn't take long to figure out who was ethical and who was a crook.

I learned a great deal from the crooks. In fact, they are the reason that I became a strong consumer advocate. Thanks to them, I have helped write and encourage new consumer protection laws. Thanks to them, I have branched off into a new career, as a radio show host, offering free advice and helpful hints on how to avoid and correct appliance problems. Thanks to them, I have hit the lecture circuit, alerting consumers to fraud, scams and rip-offs.

Those frauds, scams and rip-offs often target our senior citizens, who grew up in a time when a handshake meant something. When caring for your neighbor meant just that. When trust was prevalent and a person's word was his bond. Because our seniors are so trusting, it makes life—and fraud—so easy for the unethical service companies.

Old hockey players like me think about life in terms of a game where the smarter, more skilled players win. And we always aim for the goal. My goal in writing this book, hosting my talk show and speaking to groups is not to scare you and make you want to head for the hills. My goal is to make you a smarter consumer, one who is aware of the perils and pitfalls within the business world. My goal is to educate you so that your home life is easier, more enjoyable and free of as many mechanical hassles as possible. And one last goal: to make you chuckle now and then, scratch your head and share the challenge that the business world offers consumers today.

So...Just Who Am I Anyway?

They call me the Appliance Doctor, although once some columnist referred to me as the Gladiator of the Appliance Industry and I rather liked that. However, my real name, is Joe Gagnon (rhymes with Cannon).

I was born in Timmons, Ontario in 1941. When Canada entered the war (World War II, that is, for the younger set), both of my parents went off to Europe with the Army, leaving me, at the age of eight months, with my grandparents and nine uncles living in a farmhouse twenty-two miles from our small town in northern Canada. It was a place where people are born with hockey skates on.

I was six years old and only spoke French when my parents returned from the war. My father sent me to an English-speaking school where life was tough for the first few years. I managed to beat up enough English kids to hold my own and then I had to fight the French kids, who called me a traitor for playing with the English. But all in all, I had a great upbringing, surrounded by nature and the love of a large family and many friends.

After high school, I was determined to become a professional hockey player...but the Navy was more interested in me than any hockey league. I spent five years in the Canadian Navy, then migrated to the States in the early 1960s.

I moved to Lansing, enrolled in Michigan State University and majored in girls—until the university convinced me that I might have better things to do with my life. I played hockey for the Lansing Senators and then went to the minors with the Eastern Hockey League. Hockey was in my blood—and still is. I still play several times a week and try to participate in as many Detroit Red Wings Old-Timers games as I can make.

Marriage and five children in rapid succession forced me to settle down and get a real job. I spent the 1970s working with a major home appliance manufacturer by the name of Amana, then purchased my own appliance sales and service business. One of the finest and most ethical men I have ever met, Charles Carmack, was retiring after 30 years in the business and he taught me all that I needed to know so that I could take care of our customers to the best of my ability.

In 1984, I began a part-time radio career. Gradually, I was interviewed on other stations across the country, talking about the appliance industry and consumer fraud issues. Eventually, I moved to "the top of the golden tower" in the Fisher Building in Detroit, on Newstalk 760 WJR. I am one lucky guy to be doing my show on this great station. Not bad for a kid who couldn't speak English when he was six years old.

In 1993, I decided to write a book that I titled *Appliance First Aid*. I wrote about the small repairs consumers could perform on their appliances and discussed maintenance issues that could prevent the need for repairs. At about the same time, I started writing a weekly newspaper column for the Observer & Eccentric Newspaper chain, discussing anything having to do with appliances and the repair industry.

After warning listeners and readers about a world full of scams and fraud for years, I am absolutely convinced that we need steel-strong consumer safety legislation to regulate the American business world and to protect the American consumer. The appliances that fill our homes should not only provide us with many useful years of service, but also ensure a safe existence. There are too many home-based tragedies due to sloppy manufacturing processes, cost-cutting or ignorance. My goals are to improve consumer awareness, make the manufacturers responsible for producing fine products, and improve the safety conditions in a home.

I wrote this book because you and I are both aware of the fact that the products in our home cost a lot of money. I want to help you choose them well and maintain them well, so that they serve you for many years. I will also help you choose reputable service technicians to repair them well.

During the decade when my attention spread to public speaking and consumer affairs, my three sons went into the appliance business. In fact, one of them bought my store from me. And, just as so many wonderful things were happening to me professionally, my life turned around after a devastating divorce. I met a wonderful woman named Valorie Williams who is the mother of a wonderful little girl named Hollie. After nearly a decade-long courtship, on

New Year's Eve 1999, we married and I instantly became a father all over again. I have cherished the opportunity to help raise a lovely and bright young woman. My first book was dedicated to my first five children, of whom I am very proud. This book is dedicated to my youngest daughter.

Now, my friend, you know a little about me. Let's get down to business.

Do Your Homework before You Buy an Appliance and before You Have an Appliance Repaired

How to Buy an Appliance

The one question I get more than any other goes like this: "Joe, I need to buy a (fill in the blank). Which one is best?"

I automatically give the same answer: *You get what you pay for.* There is no single magic manufacturer that is all good. Many manufacturers make some high-quality models as well as some stripped down, cheaply constructed versions designed to capture the buyer whom is strictly price shopping. To them, this is a sophisticated marketing technique. To me, it comes close to suicide. The manufacturers are capitalizing on the public's gullibility and greed, people's desire and belief that it is possible to get something for almost nothing.

Let me tell you, folks, there is no such a thing as a free lunch. Cheap appliances are usually the most expensive things you can buy. The up-front cost may be low, but the repeated service calls that these appliances will require, their inefficient energy use and short appliance life will prove to be far more expensive than you would ever anticipate. *The less you pay for an appliance, the less you can expect from it.*

Millions of Americans can relate to that thought because they have lived through the experience. Historically, back in the old days, appliances were all soundly made products. America was once famous for quality manufacturing and we grew up expecting an appliance to last from 15 to 20 years, easily.

Today, many shoppers are discovering that times have changed and that their new appliances are only lasting an average of five to seven years. Why? Because they bought junk.

American consumers do not enjoy being ripped off. I certainly don't. What this means in the final analysis—if manufacturers would only understand this one fact—is that brand loyalty will be destroyed and irate consumers will turn their eyes elsewhere. European manufacturers are aware of Americans' discontent with the quality of their products. Look at how many new, foreign-made appliances you see in advertisements and photographs in home-oriented magazines. American manufacturers should pay heed to this.

This Is What I Tell Friends and Callers When They Ask Me for Advice:

• *Don't base your buying decision on your past experience with a 20-year-old appliance.* Many of the top brands have been completely redesigned and are just not made with the quality that have made them famous.

• *Read consumer magazines* to educate yourself about the features that are available.

• Before you buy, *call or stop by at two or three independent repair businesses and ask which brands they service the least.*

• *Study the most recent issue of* Consumer's Report *in which your appliance is reviewed.* I don't agree with everything it says, but this publication is the best single reference available to the smart shopper.

• *Talk to your friends and family members about their experiences.*

• Go to the store with a list of good questions.

• If you think that the salesperson is inexperienced or avoiding any answers to your questions, *call the manufacturer directly.* (See Chapter 10)

What You Need to Know about Appliance Stores

The first "modern" appliances I ever saw were gasoline-powered washing machines. They were often sold off the back end of the retailer's pick-up truck. More often than not, the salesman would demonstrate the product in the customer's home.

I have often thought that that salesperson must have been a pretty happy man. He was showing the consumer a new invention that would free women from a life of constant drudgery and revolutionize the American home. In most cases, he not only made the sale, he made friends for life. I often fantasize about how wonderful it would have been to live back in those good old days.

When American consumers go shopping, they often feel the same way that a soldier does when he enters a combat zone.

Let's try to make the job easier. We'll start with a reconnaissance.

There are basically three kinds of appliance stores: the "Mom and Pops," the flashy super store discount chains and the big department store chains.

It's sad to say, but the "Mom and Pops" are nearly extinct. They are smaller than the super store, manage to afford only a small fraction of the advertising available to super stores and have to charge a bit more. Since my store was one of these, I would also like to point out that the additional cost was often offset by the informative and friendly salesperson and by a conviction that the shop would stand behind its merchandise. The fact is that many of these small stores live off of their service departments.

The super store discount chains advertise until most people are utterly confused. The prices seem so low that it's hard to believe that they aren't the only game in town. The truth is, however, that the prices are not only good, but competitive pressures have forced the retailer to offer prices too low to make a legitimate profit on the sale. This forces the retailer and salespeople to get their profit through slick gimmicks and over-priced service contracts. (More on that later.)

The low-profit structures often make the salespeople slaves to "spiffs." "Spiffs" are direct payments from the manufacturer to the salesperson for selling specific merchandise. We continuously hear horror stories about high-pressure salesmanship, super prices on what are discovered to be last year's models, and an utter unfamiliarity with the product.

Meanwhile, the big, full-service department store chains are having their own troubles. Usually not price-competitive with the super store discount chains, many department stores have reduced their emphasis on appliances in pursuit of the higher profits associated with selling other merchandise. Other department stores have forced wage concessions, cut salaries and, in turn, the ranks of their professional sales force.

These descriptions are broad generalities, but the generalities are worth keeping in mind.

Now we'll approach the actual appliance selection itself.

There Are Several Important Things to Keep in Mind When Buying:

• *Trust your instincts.* If the salesperson greets you with respect, listens to your questions, answers your questions and gives you a feeling of confidence, treat that person like gold. If the reverse is true, *get out of there,* regardless of how good the prices seem to be.

• *Be alert to bait-and-switch advertising and sales techniques.* If you are told that the appliance that you came to see is temporarily out of stock, but that they'll give you a rain check, get out of there. You are being set up for a switch. If the salesperson shows you the advertised item and then tries to sell you a better machine, *get out of there.*

• *Price is very important, but be a little flexible.* If one store has a super price, but the other has terrific service and the difference is $25 or $50, think about your decision. The wise shopper will be willing to pay a little more to a store that seems honest and above-board.

• *Beware of service contracts.* I have yet to see one that really saved the consumer money on a home appliance. Your appliance should not break down. Period. If it does, chances are it will break down within 90 days and you can deal with it under warranty.

• *Make certain the price lists any and all installation costs.* Ask what additional parts, if any, may be required to install the machine. If the appliance is delivered and a part that was not listed is required to install it, tell the driver to put the appliance back in the box and return it to the store.

• *Do not pay in full up front.* I don't care what the store policy is. You can pay a small deposit down if you want to, but *pay in full only after the appliance has been installed, you have inspected it for defects, scratches, etc., and are satisfied that it is the appliance that you bought and it is running well.*

About Those Service Contracts

In 1992, research suggested that the consumer had a 50 per-cent chance of being ripped off by the service technicians who came into their home to repair an appliance. I think that their estimate was low.

I could spend the next 10 years writing about the service industry, but all I would get would be heartburn. And you would get bored. So, instead, I'll try to teach you the best way to buy service and I'll try to alert you to the dirty tricks of the trade.

When you start out with a service contract, you are imme-diately surrendering to the inevitable. You have decided that you are going to get a raw deal in the area of service, and it might as well be by that nice man or woman who has sold you that appliance.

Paying for service that you may never need is your prerogative. The only problem is that, if your appliance runs well through the initial warranty period, the probability is that you will not have a major service call until *after* your service contract has expired. You see, buying a service contract is like buying a guar-antee that you will pay more than you need on appliance repair.

Don't believe me? Let's compare paying for service as you need it versus a service contract.

When you buy service as you need it from a service company, you pay for the cost of the parts, the cost of the technician's time, truck, tools, equipment, advertising, overhead and a company profit.

When you buy service through a national warranty com-pany, you pay for the cost of the technician's time, truck, tools, equipment, overhead, company profit *and a commission for the salesman, a profit for the store, the cost of administering the warranty, the warranty company overhead, plus a profit for the warranty company.*

Which Will Cost You More?

Some may argue that the big companies have tremendous economies of scale and make up their costs in volume. If the playing field is equal, a service repairperson can only do so much quality work in a 40-hour week, no matter who he works for.

When a big company hires him as an independent contractor and gets his bid down to the lowest possible dollar, it just means that the worker has to run from job to job. He doesn't have the time to be thorough or make explanations to the consumer. Quality is the first casualty in this kind of environment.

Why Do People Buy Service Contracts?

I once met a senior citizen who had paid more than $1,800 on a service contract for an appliance because of intense pressure from the salesperson. Like many of us, she was afraid that something would happen to the appliance and that she would be unable to find good, honest service people when she needed them.

That scenario is repeated far too often. And it is a travesty.

I believe that there are two reasons why people buy service contracts—*pressure* and *fear.*

There are reasons for this pressure. Often much of the salesperson's income is derived from commissions on sales contracts. He or she is in danger of being fired if they do not convert a high percentage of appliance sales into service contracts. At some stores, prices are so close to cost that just about the only opportunity for profit comes from selling service contracts.

When you are buying an appliance, you are often pressured by the salesman to buy a service contract. It gets so bad that at some stores the salesperson will say the contract will be unavailable if you don't sign immediately, or might even make you sign a rejection form saying that you have been offered a warranty extension and have declined it.

If you are like most of us, you are an easy target for this pressure because you have a tremendous fear of having to get service on your appliance. Appliance service repairmen, politicians and used-car salesmen run neck-and-neck in the public trust department.

Don't Forget to Send in Those Warranty Cards!

Sometimes it seems as though we are swamped by paperwork. Our mailboxes are stuffed full of envelopes that inform us "Immediate Response Requested." Everything we buy seems to come with a stack of reading material. But at least one piece is important: your warranty card.

Ask yourself an important question: Have you sent in the registration card that came with the new product that you recently purchased?

I know, I know. Sometimes they ask questions that they have no right to ask. Sometimes you worry that your answers will be broadcast and your name and address sold to marketing firms. Still, I always send the warranty cards back and I'll tell you why. It's a government requirement that manufacturers of appliances keep a file on where their products are sold.

Back in the 1970s, if you didn't register the card for your microwave oven, you could be fined as much as $10,000. The government implemented this law not because it wanted to keep tabs on it citizens, but because it wanted to make certain that if there was ever a recall on a certain product (particularly of a serious health nature) the product manufacturer could reach the consumer.

I can tell you story after story of consumers ripped off by unethical service technicians who knew darn well that the appliance with the problem had been recalled—but the consumer didn't. So, the technicians took the money for the repairs and kept their mouths shut.

Keep sending those warranty cards back to the manufacturers. Some day you may be very glad that you did.

How Do You Learn about Product Recalls?

The warranty cards will give manufacturers a way to reach you—if you don't move or change your name. But what if you do move, taking the appliance with you? Or what if you buy an existing home?

The United States Consumer Product Safety Commission has announced that the recall of appliances and other household products will be posted next to the posters of America's Most Wanted Criminals in the U.S. Post Office. This is in an effort to get the word out, save lives and prevent injuries, explains Francia Smith, vice president of consumer affairs for the U.S. Postal Service. The Post Office estimates that more than seven million consumers visit post offices around the nation every day.

From now on, make it a habit to scan the colorful notices whenever you go in to mail a package or buy stamps. You could get more assistance than you bargained for.

My hat is off to the Postal Service.

Telephone Advice Can Save You Money

A good friend of mine faxed me a copy of a story written by the *New York Times* about Fix-It Advice By Phone. This story describes the experience of a 72-year-old lady who dropped a dust cloth into the lint filter opening of her clothes dryer.

She called for service, only to discover that it would cost her $45 or $50 just to have someone come to her door. She couldn't afford that kind of expense, so she decided to fix it herself.

The first thing she did was call the Sears Consumer Technical Advice Line. She was told right away that she would be charged $12 for the advice that she would receive over the phone. Then the technician proceeded to explain precisely what the lady had to do and how to do it. After a while she came back to the phone elated that she had removed the cloth from inside the lint trap.

She saved herself as much as $100 with this phone call, yet many in the service industry, including myself, have been quick to criticize those who charge for telephone advice. My business, which was founded by Mr. Carmack in the 1950s, has been giving advice free of charge long before the big boys started doing it. Still, I recognize the fact that Sears is doing a service for countless people and that the company has to pay people to answer the telephone lines.

Sears established its toll-free number (1-800-469-4643) in 1993 and has 200 technicians working the phone lines. For the $12 fee, consumers are allowed to call back as many times as needed within a 30-day period to discuss the problem.

I predict that this kind of service will grow in the years ahead and you can expect more companies to get involved. As long as the costs remain reasonable and the program truly helps do-it-yourselfers, I'm for it.

Web Sites Offer Parts for Repairs

There are times when things happen so fast that it's almost impossible to keep up. I was recently called and asked to visit the site of a new business called RepairClinic.com, in Canton. I was amazed at what I saw: a warehouse facility a block long filled with appliance parts. The computer network and web site is out of this world.

They sell parts for a living and how they do it is amazing to an old-timer like me.

Let's say you have a noise in your refrigerator and you don't know what it is. You log on to the web site and type in the product category and your complaint. The computer screen then describes what moving parts are involved and the possible noises that they are making. At this point, you type in your model number and answer some questions. The web site not only diagnoses the problem, but it shows you the part number and a picture of it. Then it gives you the price and the best way to ship it to you. In addition, the company includes a warranty on the part.

Talk about the new wave of the future! My visit left me breathless. Check them out.

How to Find Honest, Reputable and Skilled Repairmen

If you did your homework before you purchased your appliance, then you have already contacted two or three independent service companies and have asked their opinions about which brands and models they repair the least. That's a good starting point.

One of the people you spoke with was probably head and shoulders above the rest, giving you honest answers and going out of his or her way to help. If I were looking for service, he or she would be the first one who I would consider.

I would also ask all my friends and neighbors who they use and what their experiences have been. Keep in mind though, that not every customer is the same. And when you ask about experiences, ask about price.

The next place that I'd consider is the store where I bought the appliance. After all, if the store has a service department, they will be doing all the repair work while the appliance is under warranty. They should be experts on the product.

The next place to look is in the Yellow Pages. Let your fingers do the walking through the "Appliance" section, then through the sections that list appliances by name (dishwashers, ranges, refrigerators, etc.) Some of these entries will have big, fancy ads with big, fancy promises, such as free service calls.

Remember, advertising can be deceptive. It is the *customer*, not the advertiser, who pays for the advertising. The bigger the ads, the greater the cost. There are some companies that live up to their ads—but how can you tell which ones they are?

There Are Three Ways That the Unwary Consumer Can Get Fooled:

• *Local phone numbers.* They provide a legitimate consumer connection. You don't have to pay for long-distance phone calls and you take heart in the idea that you will be supporting a local business.

• *Manufacturers' names and logos.* When you see these famous, highly advertised national names and symbols, the implication is that the service company is a factory-authorized repair center. That is—and should be—a real confidence-builder. However, in the real world, many repair companies listing the top national brands are not only not factory-authorized repair centers, but they are actually illegally using the names or symbols, often without the manufacturer knowing about it. All it takes is one unscrupulous person to deceive a truckload of consumers.

• *Free service calls.* Nothing but a puppy's love is free. Sometimes an ad will promise that if you have your product repaired by the service firm after they have diagnosed the problem, they will not charge for the service call or travel costs. Translation: They have loaded those charges into their repair costs. To my knowledge, the cost of the service vehicle, fuel, insurance, tools, equipment, uniforms and the technician's hourly wage have never been paid for by the tooth fairy. No matter what the ad says, these costs must be factored into every service call. Somebody has to pay: you.

When You Make the Phone Call

When you call the company, the treatment that you receive is a good indication of the character of the company. Are they rude? Do they fumble for a scrap of paper to take down your name? Are they unresponsive? Do you repeatedly get an answering machine?

If that is the response you get on the phone, imagine getting it in person. Trust your instincts when talking to service personnel on the telephone.

Keep in mind, too, that when you make the call, the telephone is a two-way instrument. While you are sizing them up, they are sizing you up. *Your demeanor can make a big difference in the cost of the service call.* If you act tough, rough and rude on the call or in person, a professional service technician might decide, "Don't get mad. Get even."

When You Call, Here Are Some Basic Questions to Ask:

• *Ask what the charge will be.* You want a complete explanation. Is there a basic minimum? Is there a charge for travel time? Does the company make a flat charge per job or will they charge by the hour and break down the time into 15-minute intervals?

• *Ask if the company has insurance.* You want to know about product liability, property damage, bonding and worker's compensation. (Your Homeowners' Policy should cover you. But it is always better to be safe than sorry. Tell them to bring a copy of the insurance certificate with them when they come.)

• *Describe your problem to the best of your ability and ask whether they carry the parts that may need replacing.*

• *Before making the appointment, call the Better Business Bureau and the Attorney General's Office* to see if the company that you have selected has any black marks against it. Of course, if you are standing up to your ankles in water, I realize you may feel obliged to skip this step.

If given the option of a flat fee or an hourly one, an hourly fee will probably be your best bet. Flat fees are based on a relatively slow output plus a guaranteed profit. A good technician works much faster than the job is rated.

How to Prepare for a Service Call
Preparation for the call is very important—it can save you time, money and misunderstandings.

There are too many dishonest technicians around these days. Last year, I interviewed one who had scammed customers for years. He told me that when he found a broken wire in the mechanical part of the washing machine, he would quote a price of $180 for replacing the motor, then he would yank the old motor out, carry it to his truck, dust it off, put it in a box, bring it back into your house and reinstall it. Presto! The washer was fixed and he was $180 richer.

A bad guy will not take the chance that you know what he is doing. His greatest enemy is a wary consumer. If you're on the lookout, he'll do the repair as quickly as possible and move on to someone who is not as smart as you are.

Now, keep in mind that I don't want to give a bad rap to the entire service industry. Many fine people work for these companies around the country. When you find a company that is reputable and fair, treat the people like gold. Recommend them to friends. Be loud in your praise. A good act always comes back to you.

Tips to Keep in Mind before and during the Service Call:

• *Keep the paperwork for your appliances in a convenient spot.* Know what your warranty says before the appointment. If the appliance is under warranty, you need to know that. You may be eligible for at least partial payment on the parts.

• When the technician arrives, *review the warranty with him.* The technician may know of an extension or of a recall that you aren't aware of. And, I hate to admit it, but more service technicians than I want to admit try to ignore the warranty, thinking that they'll get away with it. Manufacturers pay a much lower rate for warranty work, you see.

• *Don't get dressed up for the technician.* Many service people have been trained by their companies to evaluate your financial condition by your appearance and the looks of your house. The better you look, the bigger the charge may be.

• *Show the technician the problem, then sit down and watch while he or she decides on the solution.* Don't give the technician the third degree, but do ask for an explanation of what will be done.

• If you decide to give the go-ahead, *sit back and watch.* A good, honest person won't mind. And you may learn enough to do the repair yourself the next time.

• When parts are replaced, *try to make certain that the parts installed are new,* unless you specifically approved the use of other parts.

• When the repair is complete, *keep the old parts.* Do not allow the technicians to take the old parts with them. Watch carefully. A bad guy will try to ruin a replaced part before he leaves it with you. If fraud did take place, you'll want the old parts as evidence.

Think about It: What Will You Do with Your Old Appliance?
Do you ever stop and wonder about what happens to the many millions of used major home appliances that are discarded every year?

States like Massachusetts and Minnesota are beginning to go beyond idle speculation. They are doing something about it. But Japan is the leader of the movement to recycle used appliances rather than just allowing them to fill landfills.

In Japan, a law has been passed mandating that all home appliance and electronics equipment that are no longer in use must be recycled. The original manufacturer is responsible for compliance with the law and they are building recycling plants around the country. You can bet your bottom dollar that they'll find a way to make this profitable. As it stands now, the consumer who is getting rid of a product pays $44.

Now, in the old days, little Mom and Pop service repair

establishments like the one I bought from Mr. Carmack recycled long before we thought of it as recycling. We rebuilt used appliances and sold them at significantly reduced costs, giving the product a good warranty. We helped out thousands of consumers who couldn't afford to spend $500 on a new washer. We also removed usable parts and resold them as used parts to do-it-yourselfers. That put a lot of smiles on consumers' faces.

By doing that, we also knew that if we went out on a service call and needed a part for an older product whose manufacturer no longer stocked that particular part, we had the whereabouts to pull the part from an older machine in the back yard.

People are opting to buy new appliances rather than fix them, as we did in years past—and I think that it's a crying shame that we are treating expensive appliances like a hair curler or a toaster. Think about it: How many times have you heard consumers or repair people say, "The cost of parts is so expensive for major home appliances that we aren't bothering to fix it. We'll buy new."

The move to recycle rather than to discard and buy new is an idea whose time has come—again.

It seems that all good ideas go around and then come back again.

Calendar

The Care and Maintenance of Your Appliances: What to Do and When to Do It

January
• When the weatherman forecasts temperatures below 0 degrees, open all cupboard doors around sinks and other pipes. This allows heat circulation in the areas that might need it the most.

• Make a New Year's resolution to clean the condenser under your refrigerator every four months. As you may have noticed, cats and dogs like to lie beside your refrigerator because of the heat that it emits—and in return they emit hair and dust. The debris that covers all the black tubing under a refrigerator is the biggest source of service calls for refrigerators and it can cause premature failure of the compressor, poor temperatures and an increase of $5 to $10 on your monthly utility bill. Hardware stores sell refrigerator condenser brushes that allow you to clean the coils properly. Pull the plug on the refrigerator. Use the brush and thoroughly clean the coils. When you move the refrigerator back in place, making sure that it is far enough from walls and cabinets. A clean condenser will add years of life to your refrigerator.

February

• Beware of fires caused by candles lit during a romantic Valentine's Day dinner. Make sure that your special night is safe as well as romantic.

• Never leave a fire burning in the fireplace while you are out of a room for long periods of time.

March

• At least two weeks before Easter or Passover, clean your stove and oven. Then check them to make sure that everything is operating. If your range is gas, make sure you crack open a kitchen window while you are using it. (Gas ranges are known to give off carbon monoxide and introducing a little fresh air into the house can prevent the problem.) Make sure that the automatic igniter inside a gas oven is lighting the flame each time it cycles. And, for goodness sake, don't slam the door too hard. Igniters are so fragile that something as simple as closing the door too hard could break them.

• If you use a warm wash setting on the washing machine, it's time to shut off the cold water valve just slightly. Make the adjustment using a candy thermometer so that the water in your washer tub is *exactly* 100 degrees.

• Give your dishwasher a Tang breakfast treatment. Purchase the powdered Tang from your grocery store. Make sure that you turn on the hot water at the sink faucet first. Let the dishwasher run for three or four minutes, then shut it off and open the door. Deposit the entire contents of the Tang container into the dishwasher; close the door and let the machine run through the entire cycle. This will clean out all the undissolved soap build-up and your dishwasher will work like new.

April
• Clean your refrigerator condenser with a brush.
• When you are sure that the last snow has fallen, drain the gasoline out of your snowblower and dispose of it properly. Take the snowblower into the shop for cleaning and maintenance.
• Change the filters in your furnace and shut off the humidifier. This is a good time to clean the humidifier and throw away the old filter. Replace the filter every year with a new one. Remember, bacteria grow in old filters—even filters that you think you've cleaned thoroughly.
• Check to make sure refrigerator and freezer doors seal properly and that the appliances are far enough away from walls or cabinets.
• Spring and summer storms can cause havoc with our appliances and electronic equipment. Power surges can create nightmarish situations. Purchase surge protectors and install them on appliances, hot water heaters, electronic equipment and computers. You might show your family members how to shut off the main circuit breaker in your home during power outages. It should be switched back on after the power has been restored to your area.

May

• Prepare your lawn tools for the gardening season, using Brillo pads to remove any rust.

• Try out your lawnmower, edger, trimmer, rototiller and leaf blower to make sure that everything is working properly and that the blades are sharp.

• Put the nozzle on the garden hose and remove any winter debris from the outside condenser. Clean it well, spraying it thoroughly.

• Turn on your outside water spigots.

• Check your lawn irrigation systems.

• In the first few days of warm weather, check your air conditioning system. Set the wall thermostat to 80 degrees and switch on the AC/ON setting—without switching on the compressor outside. Many compressors have a built-in heater that will warm up the oil in the bottom of the compressor; this is especially important when the evenings are still cool. Sometimes the thick cool oil will damage the compressor—and that will result in expensive repairs. So don't set the thermostat so the compressor comes on. Just switch on the setting to AIR to check and prepare the system.

• If you have room air conditioners, take them to the car wash and hose them down thoroughly. With enough pressure you'll be able to clean the inside of the unit without taking it apart. Spray the front and back and the louvers on the side. Most of the damage to a room air conditioner is caused by dirt build-up inside the shiny condenser in the rear. A good cleaning will allow the conditioner to function just as good as the day it was made. Millions of consumers will buy a new air conditioner this year and, believe me, many wouldn't have to if they would attend to a little maintenance.

June

• Take advantage of the warm summer mornings to prepare for winter. Caulk windows, paint woodwork.

• Take a toothbrush and clean the hinges on the dryer vent line flapper outside. Every year people pay big money for a repairman to remove the litter and creatures who sought warmth from the cold over the winter months.

• In preparation for the hot summer months when you won't feel like cooking as much, thoroughly clean microwave oven, stove top and oven.

• Check washing machine hoses at the point where the metal pieces are at the ends. Any sign of corrosion means that you need new hoses. A ruptured hose can cause terrible damage to a home.

July

• Before your chimney sweep gets booked for the fall, make an appointment to have your chimney cleaned and your furnace vents checked. This is their slow time.

• Fill your garbage disposal full of ice cubes and let it stand that way for at least one hour. Then switch on the disposal with cold water running and let it operate for at least three minutes.

• Meanwhile, fill a bowl of water and let it boil in your microwave oven. (Make sure that the bowl is appropriate for microwave use.) Remove the bowl and use paper towels and Windex to thoroughly clean the appliance, inside and out. Check to make sure that the microwave has no objects on top or around it that would block its air circulation.

• Install a surge protector on the wall outlet for the microwave.

August

- Clean your refrigerator condenser coils with a brush.
- This may seem premature, but you'll be glad you planned ahead. Turn on your heater and make sure that it works properly. Have your vents and your duct work cleaned.
- Clean your stove top and your oven.
- Give your dishwasher a Tang treatment.

September

- Clean out the clothes dryer's vent, which directs air to the outside. Make sure that you are not using a plastic or tinfoil vent line because it can be very dangerous. Take an old toothbrush and clean the hinges on the flapper door outside. When that little door fails to close all the way, critters who want to escape Mother Nature's cold months can be attracted by the warmth. To prevent this, spray the surface of the outside flapper with an insect repellent used for ants and bees. DO NOT put a nylon sock or screen over the vent exits; this will restrict the air and create a lint build-up inside the vent line—which will become a serious fire hazard. Cold air will also be drawn into your laundry room—and the end result is a waste of energy because the dryer drum is now ice cold. That can add as much as ten minutes to the drying time of each load of laundry.
- Use a candy thermometer and make sure that the temperature of water in your washing machine reaches 100 degrees when the machine is set for warm water wash. Your laundry will not be washed properly unless your machine reaches that temperature. You can adjust the water temperature by slowly closing off the cold water faucet and checking the temperature until you reach the right one.

• Take your room air conditioners and dehumidifiers to the car wash and hose them down completely. *Don't* turn them on afterwards, when they are wet. Put them away until next summer and notice how much better they work. And remember: Heating, cooling and dehumidifying products should never be tipped sideways or upside down. Also remember: They must stand in their installation position for a few hours before plugging them in.

• Once you have removed air conditioning units from your windows, check the windows to make sure they close properly, and keep cold air out when they need to.

• Prepare your snowblower for winter: Change the oil, make sure that the spark plug and wire are clean and firing properly.

October

• Purchase a bag or two of kitty litter to use this winter when you're stuck in a parking lot or when a friend gets stuck in your driveway. Keep one bag at home, one in the car. Throwing a few handfuls of kitty litter under your wheels really does help to create great traction.

• Shut off the water supply that leads to your outdoor water spigots. You do this from inside the house. You would be surprised at how much damage each year is due to frozen pipes leading to the garden hose. The plumbing industry is kept very busy each winter taking care of these unnecessary freeze-ups.

• Check your lawn mower, edger, rototiller and trimmer. Wash them down, dry them off, clean and oil them, put them away in start-up condition for next year.

• Make sure that you'll have a panic-free holiday season. There are too many panic situations when stoves and ovens refuse to work properly and turkeys remain undercooked or uncooked. Check stove burners: Make sure they are clean. Test each burner by setting the different controls to low, medium and high. If your burners pull out, check to see if the ends are corroded. The ends should be shiny and free of pit marks; if not, replace the burner and burner blocks. *Check your ovens*: Insert a hanging oven thermometer (which can be purchased at any hardware store) into your oven and set the temperature for 350 degrees. If the thermometer indicates any variation of 25 degrees or less, adjust your baking by raising or lowering the oven temperature knob accordingly. Otherwise, repair the range. The service industry becomes very busy just before the holidays and if parts must be ordered, you may be out of luck if you wait too long.

November

• The greatest number of automobile and pedestrian accidents occur the first time the roads freeze and during the first snowfall. We are accustomed to summer driving and we fail to realize that our reflexes, like our clothing, must change for winter. Before you take off on the first day of ice or snow, why not drive around the neighborhood a few times *slowly*, to get the feel of things?

• Prepare your lawnmower for winter. Remove gasoline— making sure to dispose of it properly. Have blades sharpened and any necessary maintenance done.

• Check all holiday lights for faulty wiring

December

• Make sure this will be a safe and happy holiday. Don't leave decorative lights on at night or while you are away from the house. Every year, without fail, families suffer the tragedy of death because holiday lights are plugged in or used improperly.

• *To all my readers and friends, a special winter warning:* Don't suffer the agony and pain of a broken ankle or hip this winter. The dictionary defines "agony" as "a death struggle" and in too many cases, that is what an accident can become. Forget fashion, wear boots with good, thick treads. When my parents were alive, I made sure that they wore a pair of muck lugs that had enough tread to stop on an ice rink. You ladies out there who worry that your legs or ensemble won't look very nice in a big pair of boots should remember this: It's better to be smiling and standing up than crying and lying down.

Back to the Basics: Building an Enviroment for Successful Living

Start at the Ground Level

If you are fortunate enough to build your dream home, don't just focus on the type of siding, the wood available for kitchen cabinets and the colors of the walls. Build a home that will allow you to live comfortably and safely, bypass common building nightmares and save money with energy-efficient designs and appliances.

I know of a community where several new homes were built with foolish, and downright dangerous, designs. They have the dryer vented into and up the walls and across the attic °much too long and consumers are forced to use that dreaded—and dangerous—plastic vent line. This builder did something unconscionable, without any thought for his homeowners' safety or the state construction codes, which specify that a vent line should be no longer than 14 feet and should be metal.

I would sincerely hope that the construction industry would wise up to how many house fires are started each year by an improperly vented clothes dryer.

Hundreds of thousands of homes are built each year with laundry rooms located somewhere other than the basement. You find them in the kitchen, off the kitchen or even on the top floor of a multi-story home. And when you do, you hear people complaining about the vibrations when a washer goes through a spin cycle. Or the way the washer and dryer thump and dance around the room. Why won't builders understand the very best flooring for appliances is cement? These problems are going to get worse, folks. I can't begin to estimate how many service calls covered by warranty are being performed today when nothing is wrong but the location and flooring.

Exasperated by what I see all around me, I've put some thought into ways I would renovate an existing home or build a new one. Some of these ideas are far from the norm. I thought that you might want to know what I consider a well-built house:

• Let's start with the dryer. *I would have a direct hole made on the wall behind the dryer* so that venting the appliance would be as quick and efficient as possible. The hole would be in the exact position where the exhaust comes out of the dryer so that a short piece of solid aluminum vent line would fit perfectly in place. This method would add years of use to the appliance because it would assure the homeowner that little lint would be able to remain within the line.

• Let's move on to kitchen floor. *I would make certain that the sub-board was removable in front of the dishwasher.* I can't tell you how many times people purchase a new dishwasher and when they try to remove the old one, it won't come out. There are leveling legs on a dishwasher and they go up only so far. If they don't clear the new floor, it often means that the kitchen counter top must be removed. That can end up costing more than the dishwasher.

• *I would have a circuit breaker box installed in the stairway leading into the basement.* Every year in this country, home-owners are killed when they step into a flooded basement. I would make it easy to switch off all power to the home quickly and safely. I would also place a smoke alarm there.

• *The plumbing pipes to my clothes washer would have the new shut-offs called handies. Unlike the traditional round turning handles, these make it easy to shut off water supply.* Too much damage to homes is caused by ruptured hoses leading to a clothes washer—and it will only happen to you once before you give this some serious thought.

• I would make sure that *all gas lines have a shut-off valve installed where I can reach it easily,* in case of an emergency.

• Behind my refrigerator, I would have louvers cut into the wall and even a small fan installed to remove the heat that is displaced by the refrigerator compressor. This is critical to the refrigerator's life expectancy and also to the cost of operating the refrigerator.

• *I would place the stove and microwave far enough away from the refrigerator* that the refrigerator didn't suffer the added heat from cooking and baking.

• *I would situate the washer on a cement floor.* A wood floor will take only so much abuse from the repeated vibrations of a spin cycle before trouble begins.

Small Ways You Can Save Big

Savings come in all sizes and in many different ways. You can save yourself money and aggravation by reducing your use of electricity or gas. Esther Shapiro, an expert in the field, suggests that you might consider experimenting with some common and commonsense ways to save energy and money. For instance:

• Reduce your use of the kitchen stove. Eat cold foods and sandwiches more often.

• Prepare foods that take less time (and therefore less energy).

• Pay attention when cooking and baking—don't overcook.

• Cook everything one way or another—everything in the oven or everything on top of the stove.

• Stir-fry your meats and vegetables. They can be prepared faster and they can actually be healthier for you.

• If you like hot beverages during the day, make a big pot of coffee or tea in the morning and put the rest in a thermos bottle.

• For iced tea, use the sun as a heat source. Put several tea bags in a jar filled with cold water and screw on the lid. Set it out in the sun for a few hours until the tea looks strong enough to drink. Then add ice cubes.

• Use the minimum amount of water to cook your food. Put in just enough to keep it from scorching. Let vegetables steam cook.

• Use tight-fitting lids to reduce cooking time.

• Use pots and pans with flat bottoms and straight sides, so they fit the burners.

• Buy shiny and bright pots and pans.

• Use a pressure cooker for faster cooking.

• Never fill a teakettle or any other container with more water than you are going to use.

• Use cold water to boil water. The energy used for heating cold water is less than the energy used by the water heater to maintain warm water.

• Clean out the scale in kettles. Hard water deposits can reduce heat transfer.

• Keep burners clean and burner pots unplugged for more efficient cooking.

• Keep reflectors or drip pans clean so they will bounce back more heat to the bottom of your pan.

• When cooking with electricity, get in the habit of turning off burners several minutes before the allotted time. The heating element will stay hot enough to finish the cooking.

• Use high heat settings to bring water to a boil or start cooking foods with water, then reduce the heat to a desired lower setting. But don't set an electric surface unit on "high" if you're just warming something.

• If you buy a new range, get one with a thermostatically controlled burner (burner with a brain), where the heat is automatically reduced to maintain the selected temperature.

• Expand the family menus to include stews and other single dish meals that can be prepared in a slow cooker or crock-pot.

What to Do in an Emergency

What Should You Do Once Flood Waters Recede?

Spring is always a wake-up call for nature. Birds return to the trees and skies. The sap begins to flow. Our thoughts turn to the outdoors. Sometimes, however, the outdoors comes indoors, thanks to fast-melting snow, fast-rushing rivers and streams and ice-blocked water mains and lines.

Several years ago, the mayor of Westland, Robert J. Thomas, stopped by my store and asked me to speak to several hundred homeowners gathering that evening as a result of the many flooded basements in one of the area's subdivisions. I was invited to speak about the risk factors involved when appliances are submerged in water.

The first thing to worry about when a basement floods is the danger of electrical shock. That occurs when an area has water and electricity coming together—and the result can kill you. If you walk through several inches of water and touch anything, the electrical charge will have completed a circuit through your body and you'll shine like a light bulb.

The safest procedure to follow in case of a flooded basement is to call someone who knows what he's doing.

Appliances have motors that must be dried out *completely* before you turn them back on. It isn't enough just to let them stand for a few days. You must direct a fan on the motor for days or repeatedly use a hair dryer to blow them dry. Motors and compressors have areas where water will accumulate and you can't see those spots.

Some clothes dryers, furnaces and hot water heaters have gas valves that are very fragile. The internal workings will not stand any kind of corrosion. Introducing water into a gas valve may not be a cause for immediate alarm, but what can happen months or years down the road can be one heck of an explosion. It is crucial that you replace the gas valve—that is the only sure way to safeguard your home.

You see, even though gas valves are sealed, they still have an orifice that allows gas to exit and burn during operation. Water can enter this orifice, corrode the valve and eventually force that valve to stay in the open position when it should automatically close. As a result, the gas would pour out of the valve and cause a deadly situation. My company had a strict policy that we would not go into a home and fix gas appliances without changing the gas valves.

Don't take chances. Change a valve. And perhaps you'll save your life.

A Simple Solution to Frozen Pipes

In this part of the world, we sometimes have winter temperatures drop to some pretty bone-chilling degrees. And if our cars, noses, toes and roads can freeze, so can the plumbing in our homes.

Every winter, thousands of homeowners will hear the heart-stopping sound of running water in their homes, only to discover after a frantic search that the noise is coming from a broken and frozen water pipe. It's the kind of thing that generally occurs only one time in a homeowner's life—because once is too often.

This is a fairly typical scenario:

It's the middle of the night and you awaken to the sound of running water. You run downstairs and discover water pouring all over the place. You pinch yourself to wake up because what you see looks like the upper deck of the *Titanic*. Then you dash around looking for a valve to shut off the flood. As much as you try, you cannot budge the water valve. As you make your way quickly to the main valve on the water meter, you ask yourself worriedly, "When was the last time I ever worked the valves, to make sure they could open and close?"

After trying to close the main water valve leading into the house and realizing that you can't budge this one either, you get out the old pipe wrench. You wrap the wrench around the handle, pull with all your might and finally you feel something move.

Bang!!!

The entire pipe breaks off in your hand. Water is pouring into your home and you start to wonder about life jackets.

This has now become a potential life-and-death situation.

Don't let this happen to you!

Late in the fall, before frosts are a daily occurrence, go downstairs and shut off the valves that lead to the outside water spigots. Wrap a piece of insulation around the line where it goes through the wall and make sure you drain the line by opening and closing the outside spigot.

If the valves are all corroded and difficult to turn, the smartest thing to do is to have them replaced. Ask a plumber to install a new kind of shut-off that can be done with the pressure of a finger.

If you should happen to think that this will never happen to you, call a plumber and ask what it's like to crawl around in spaces where the temperature has dropped into the below-zero range, when they work 24-hour shifts and still have people frantically calling them.

And I haven't yet mentioned the dollars involved if you neglect to do this very simple procedure.

The Tragedies of Gas Leaks

When I was a young man working in a factory, we workers would look out the windows of the cafeteria as we ate our lunches. One day, some residents who lived across the street from the plant returned home from their vacation. When they walked into the house, they turned on a kitchen light. The arc inside the light bulb was enough to ignite gas that had leaked from an appliance line. The entire house was sent flying. Debris soared higher than the branches of 100-year-old elm trees. Three people perished in that tragedy.

Consumers must understand the role of gas appliances and the way they work. It is a life-and-death matter to make sure that a gas dryer is installed properly. The dryer should have a length of copper tubing that runs from the black iron pipe or fitting all the way to the dryer. In order to clean and service the machine, there should be a coiled-up piece of copper tubing three or four feet long so that you can move the dryer away from the wall. The gas vent line should be metal, not plastic, and the dryer area should be clean and free of all debris.

What about the gas range in the kitchen? Shouldn't that have a long copper wire too, so you can pull the range out in order to service it or paint the wall?

In days not so long ago, we in the service industry always used copper tubing to install gas stoves and dryers because copper is solid and cutting a hole through it takes a hacksaw. A clothes dryer vibrates as it operates and any rubbing creates a noise that draws enough attention that you will take care of the situation immediately. Even though the gas range has very little movement, I have always believed that the safest method of getting gas to it was by using copper tubing there, too.

But what happened in the service industry is that manufacturers and technicians became lazy and many times decided to take the shortest route to get something done. A few years ago the stainless steel and plastic-coated gas lines were invented. Flexible and sold in different lengths, it became the product to use for gas companies and service industries. I didn't believe in them then and I still don't.

Ask city inspectors to name a state code that permits such lines and they won't be able to do it. If a piece of connector is flexible, then it's not solid, and that means that they can cause the kind of explosion that I witnessed so many years ago. What kind of gas line do you have in your home? It is crucial that you find out—and replace it if it's the wrong kind.

Someone told me the other day that carbon monoxide detectors sold in stores carry a recommendation that they not be installed in kitchens. My guess is that the manufacturer knows that some gas ranges cause carbon monoxide to accumulate in the kitchen. For this reason, I have always recommended that your kitchen windows be open when you are cooking—that pretty well takes care of the carbon monoxide problem caused by gas ranges. Now I'm recommending that everyone install a carbon monoxide detector in the kitchen, just in case.

It could save your life.

Seething about Surges?
Are We Helpless during Brownouts?

I had returned from a five-day vacation in California and had just sat down to read back issues of the newspaper when the headlines caught my attention. They said that Detroit Edison didn't have enough energy to pass out to every home, so the company had decided to cut back on the amount of voltage they would send across the wires.

This is an old problem that dates back to the 1970s. Now it resurfaces with new ramifications, thanks to the tremendous number of electronics and appliances we have in our homes nowadays.

Back then, it was hard for Edison to admit that any home was not being supplied with the correct amount of voltage. Consequently, many refrigerator compressors burned up because of low-voltage situations. In those days, the consumer footed the bill. Now we know better, and it is imperative that the proper voltage be supplied to our homes.

Low voltage supplies to a home can cause serious and costly problems. When you see light bulbs suddenly dim, television pictures get smaller and you hear motors suddenly operating with a strained sound, it is time for you to shut off those products. I repeat: *In a brownout situation, shut off your electrical and electronic equipment.* Brownouts can result in some very expensive repairs.

Motors, compressors and electronics are designed to operate on 100 volts. Even a simple drop of 10 volts can damage these machines beyond reasonable repairs. If your compressor failed today, would you be able to prove that it was a low-voltage condition that caused the failure? Will your electric company pay for the cost of replacements and repairs?

Perhaps your insurance company will cover the cost of some of the repairs. My insurance man tells me that I have $1,000 worth of coverage for such a happening. It won't take care of everything in the worst cases, but it will help. You might want to inquire about special riders available through your insurance company.

Let me tell you what I do during a power outage. I shut off the main fuse box and I don't turn it back on until 15 minutes or so after the power has been restored to my home. I let things level off in the neighborhood and then I flip the switch back on.

Make things easier for yourself and for your neighbors. When lightening storms flash and you realize the power is beginning to falter, shut off the main fuse box. And, at times of peak demand for electricity during the hottest months of summer, shut off the air conditioning if you plan to be gone all day. If enough of us did that, the energy savings would be tremendous—let alone the savings in potential repairs.

∾

During storms and high winds, you'll hear news reporters telling us to pull the plugs on appliances, keep the freezer door closed, watch for frozen power lines and do all the common-sense things that are needed to keep your family and your home safe. You won't however, hear much conversation about power surges or brownouts that occur after the power has been restored to your home. These two things are devastating to appliances and those of us in the service industry are kept very busy after a storm.

I don't understand why people can bury cable television lines, gas lines and phone lines underground, yet there is little talk of burying all electricity lines beneath the ground. So many tragedies occur when electrical lines come down and cease to function.

A power surge can fry your computer or television set, the compressor in your refrigerator and central air conditioner—and just about everything else that runs off electricity. *You need a surge protector on every appliance.* Better yet, contact an electrician about having a whole-house surge protector installed at the fuse box.

Surge protectors were invented fairly recently. Although they are relatively inexpensive to buy, they can save your appliances, televisions, electronics, and computers and just about anything else that runs on electricity.

The Brown family, who lives near me, learned the hard way why we need surge protectors. During a storm when electricity was jumping across the night skies, a power surge took place at the Browns' home. By some quirk of fate, the only product to suffer damage was their beautiful, large new television set. Off it went to the repair shop for damage repairs and in a few days it returned, as good as new, with a substantial repair bill.

Several days later, I saw Mrs. Brown again, and once again she mentioned that her television was in the repair shop. Another storm had passed through and another power surge had hit her house. Again the television was zapped. I asked her if she had a surge protector on that particular electrical outlet and she looked puzzled.

I cannot overly stress the importance of having surge protectors installed in your homes. Save yourself the cost, heartbreak, effort and aggravation of discovering that expensive investments are beyond repair, thanks to a fluke in the electrical current.

Tips on Trips

If you are planning a trip that will take you away from your home for an extended amount of time, plan ahead to make sure you have prepared the home for the trip as carefully as you have packed your suitcase. These are some tips to make sure that your homecoming is as satisfying as any trip could be:

• If your dishwasher seal sits in a dry condition for too long, it will shrink, causing serious problems when you are ready to start the appliance up again. The dishwasher seal is made of rubber and sits on the shaft of the motor. Its job is to prevent water from leaking onto the motor when the machine is running. Some manufacturers ensure the efficiency of that seal by leaving water in the bottom of the dishwasher if it is going to sit in a warehouse for a period of time. You should do the same and have a quart of water replaced in the bottom of the machine every month you are away.

• Your garbage disposer can become a source of a foul odor. A good practice is to fill the disposer with ice cubes and citrus (lemon, orange or lime) peels. Let the mixture sit for an hour, then turn on the water and the disposer. If you are having someone check your house, have them run the disposer with water for 30 seconds or so every month.

• Your refrigerator should never be left inoperative for more than two months. Turn it off, wash out the interior, discard all food and prop the refrigerator open. When you turn it back on, let it run for several hours. Don't let your house temperature drop below 55 degrees. Temperatures below 55 degrees can cause damage to the compressor and that will mean an expensive repair bill.

• Your gas range has a shut-off valve that should be shut off when you leave. There's nothing worse than arriving home and flicking on the light switch, only to have the house blow up. That time, your trip won't be planned.

• Your hot water heater, whether gas or electric, should be shut off. The water supply line should be closed as well.

• Your washer has two hoses which come into it. When you leave, make sure the water supply is in the off position. These two fill hoses have been known to burst and cause thousands of dollars of damage. This happens too frequently all around the country. If the shiny fittings on the end of the hoses look corroded, change the hoses.

• Your clothes dryer has a vent leading to the outside. Check the flapper outside to make sure that it is closing all the way. Take a toothbrush and clean its hinges. That will prevent a critter from moving into the place and making it his home while you're away.

• Have a family friend or relative stop by and check on your home. Peace of mind is the greatest feeling.

How to Stay Warm in Winter, Cool in Summer, Hot and Wet in the Shower, and Dry during the Summer Months

Furnaces

It is a known fact that winter comes every year. And it is a known fact that the first few weeks of cold weather are the hardest weeks to get prompt service from a heating company. Their phones are ringing off the hook and everybody wants service now. Beat the rush. Be the first to recognize that winter will come, just as it always has, and you need to be ready for it—months before it actually comes.

Keep in mind that the heating and cooling industry has been very busy in the past few years—much more so than ever before. When the economy is booming and new houses are being built in record numbers, heating contractors are busy. Their installations are usually booked months in advance, so during the fall and winter seasons, homeowners might find themselves waiting longer than they would like—and certainly longer than is comfortable—to have problems fixed. *Beware of the calendar* when it comes to furnaces.

Long before the evening temperatures drop below 50 degrees, turn on your thermostats and check out your system.

Make sure that everything is working smoothly and efficiently, without funny noises, long delays in getting heat or any sign of smoke. If you notice anything wrong, call your repairman immediately. If nothing appears wrong, but you failed to take my advice and have your heating vents and ducts thoroughly cleaned in the spring, do it in the summer, weeks before the cool months descend. Especially if your furnace is 10 years old or older, call and set up an appointment.

Typically it should cost anywhere from $49 to $99.90. The technician will check your heat exchanger to see if it's leaking carbon monoxide, then lubricate and clean your blower and do other maintenance checks that should give you a winter of heated comfort. Now, this is well worth the cost, folks. Don't be taken in by the call offering you a nine-point check and cleaning for $19.95. If you do, you would have just become a fool—and the joke is on you!

This may sound cruel for me to say so, but it's true, as many consumers have admitted to me *after* they were ripped off. These rip-off companies operate on one of humanity's basic instincts—greed—to take advantage of too many people.

Beware and Be Aware!

Recently, in my mailbox at the radio station, I found a newsletter from the Independence Hills subdivision in Farmington Hills, Michigan. I sat there with my coffee and read it. I was so impressed by what I read that I think it is only fitting that I give you some of its content. I'm sure that someone out there will get a few ideas to use in their neighborhoods.

Mary Winkler wrote that her air conditioning unit had stopped working and she had a company come out and check it. They told her that the blower motor in the furnace had to be replaced. Cost: $600. But, the service man recommended that the whole furnace be replaced instead of just the motor. Cost: $2,100. Mary wisely said that she would think about it.

She has a friend who suggested that she call Family Heating and Cooling to get another price on a new furnace. Mary writes:

"I called Family Heating and Mike came out. I asked him to check it out and to give me a quote for a new furnace. By now I was convinced that a new heater would be needed.

"Let me check one more thing,' Mike said and he went to his truck for another testing device. 'If this is the problem, it will be a quick and inexpensive fix.'

"It turned out to be only the capacitator, an $18 part. The service call charge, plus parts, was $10 cheaper than the first company's vanilla do-nothing-to-solve-the-problem service call. Mike could have made a big sale. Instead, he made the extra effort and reported that it was an easy and inexpensive repair."

Three cheers for honest, ethical and capable repair people!

Because of Mary's experience with a rip-off company, the subdivision is starting a referral service for their homeowners, listing ethical roofers, floor installers, deck-washing companies, landscapers, plumbers and remodeling contractors. These folks are smart and I'm proud of what they're doing, and I highly recommend that other subdivisions or neighborhoods do the same thing. We should all work to become smarter consumers—and help our neighbors do the same.

Scams, Scams and More Scams

It is absolutely essential that we become aware of how many scams there are in the business world. The Michigan Consumer Protection Act is as useful as a bump on a log and I can't say much more about some of the people we elect to office. When will we have laws that truly protect consumers from smooth, unethical, rip-off artists? Their scams might be as simple as changing the name on the paperwork, thus gouging the unsuspecting customer, but there are a host of others.

As many of you know, Evelyn Stern, who works with Call for Action out of the offices of WXYZ-TV, has become a weekly participant on my radio show. She spends a few minutes each week describing what's happening in the world of rip-offs. You need to spend only a short time listening to this lady before you realize how much she cares about people.

Call for Action is a national organization that helps consumers around the country. They have a knowledgeable finger on the pulse of what's happening nationwide. Evelyn told a distressing story about a lady who spent $12,000 to have a new furnace installed in her home. The price should have been around $2,000, but this consumer fell for the old scare tactic used by the few unethical heating companies that want to get rich quick at the cost of the consumer.

Let me give you a typical scenario that takes place when a homeowner is ripped off by one of the unethical companies in the heating business.

Picture an elderly lady living alone. Her children are out of state. She has a nice, neat home with a fairly new car parked in the garage. It is obvious that she can take care of herself and may have a few dollars tucked away.

She receives a phone call from a heating company, which informs her that they will come out and check and clean her furnace for the low price of $29.95. "Lady," the caller says, "call any heating company and they'll tell you it should be done every couple of years. And nobody does it as cheap as we can."

She agrees to have them come to her house.

The furnace guy comes out and sprays a solution inside her furnace and has a sniffer located near the register that shows her a color indicating that she has carbon monoxide coming out of her furnace. (This test can be rigged to give a false reading.) He shows her rust and stress marks in the heat exchanger and makes her believe they are cracks. He tells her that she has to move out of the house NOW because she will surely die if she sleeps here another night.

The little lady is so frightened that she is like putty in the hands of this crook. The furnace guy is so smooth that she is ready to kiss him for saving her life. The rest of this story has been repeated thousands of times.

"Lady, I can have two guys here in the next few hours and we'll install a new furnace and have you back in business in no time. No hotel necessary. You'll be sleeping in your own bed tonight. We've got an $8,000 furnace which I can sell to seniors for $6,000—that's a pretty good deal," he tells her.

The lady is hooked and about to be ripped off.

It will be too late when she hears or reads something that triggers the idea that she might have been cheated and she calls me. If she had installed a carbon monoxide detector or called the gas company for a second opinion, this wouldn't have happened.

It is up to every consumer to be aware of possible fraud.

Here Are a Few Steps to Take to Make Sure That You Don't Fall for a Rip-off Scam:

• Check the credentials of every company that you invite into your home.

• Get more than one opinion on whether you need to replace a furnace.

• If it's necessary, get more than one estimate for a new furnace.

• Call other companies and ask what they charge for a furnace to service a home the square footage of yours.

• If you have been told that you have a leak in the heat exchanger, call the gas company to check it out.

• Remember: A good heating contractor will never use scare tactics. He will help you at the most reasonable price, with the least inconvenience to your time.

Care and Maintenance:

• On one of the first warm days of spring, replace the furnace filter and shut off the humidifier on the furnace. This is much more efficient than waiting until fall to do it.

• Replace the pad each year. I remind myself that this could have prevented the Legionnaire's Disease. That makes spending a little time and a few dollars for a new pad a reasonable expense.

• Take apart the condensate pump, which pumps the water from the furnace to a sink or drain, if your unit has one. I use white vinegar to clean it and I pour a pint of the vinegar through the system to clean the drain tubes.

• Every two years I take the furnace plenum apart and clean the A-coil, which is located inside. Use a vacuum cleaner and soft brush for this delicate task.

• In the spring, I reinstall the two cartridge fuses that I removed last fall to make sure that no one would turn on the air conditioning unit by mistake during the winter months.

• Don't wait until frost is on the ground before you call to have your furnace checked and worked on. Have vents and ducts cleaned in the spring. Turn the furnace on during August to make sure it works properly.

Air Conditioners

Plan on an Annual Check-up

Just as your furnace needs checking a month or two before you anticipate using it, so does your air conditioner. Sometime around April or May, turn your air conditioning unit on and make sure that it works properly. Don't wait until you arrive home from a hard day at work, hot, sticky and with a headache, to discover there is no way to cool your house—or your temper. Check your unit in advance.

If you do not have a central air conditioning system, remember that you can count on one thing happening every year as regularly as tax time rolls around: With any prolonged heat wave, you won't be able to find a new room air conditioner to purchase anywhere. The stores simply run out of stock.

On top of that, repairmen are hard to come by. Traditionally, the heating and air conditioning industry has been unable to handle all the service calls that come their way during the first few hot spells of the year. You can expect a waiting period before the technician arrives to fix a problem with your unit.

And on top of that, new federal laws mandate that the air conditioning industry must capture and recycle the freon in your system before it is released into the atmosphere, so new technology and training programs have been developed within the industry. The result is that costs for the consumer have risen. The message therefore is: Take care of what you have and buy new appliances carefully.

As in every business, unfortunately, there are a few unethical companies that will take consumers to the cleaners financially if they can manage it. You need to be sure about whom you call to come out to your house.

There's a Good Reason for Spring Cleaning

The first message is to take good care of the units you have. Check them regularly to make sure they are operating properly. Clean them annually—more often if they are exposed to excessive amounts of dirt and dust. If you live on a dirt road or in an area where construction projects are a way of life, your system needs to be cleaned often. Let me give you an example of why you need to do this.

Last July, on a sweltering 92-degree day, a lady pulls up to the shop door with her 12,000-BTU air conditioner in the back of her van. She needs this fixed now, she says. She's not only hot as hell, she's mad because the unit is only six months past the warranty period. The dealer won't help her and he won't even sell her another one because he ran out of air conditioners two weeks ago. She's screaming at me, blue murder, demanding that this machine be fixed while she waits. She is not leaving, she yells. Neither are the five customers who have lined up behind her to purchase a part and who are listening intently.

The phone is ringing at the rate of five times per minute and my customer won't stop ranting so I can hear the folks talking on the phone. The line behind her grows to seven people. In an effort to restore some sanity, I have two shop technicians handle the phones and I take the casing off of her air conditioner. By this time, two more people have crowded into the shop and I begin holding a seminar like the ones I do at the Silverdome or Cobo Hall. The only difference is that I get paid big bucks at those places and all I'm getting here is a lot of static.

As I'm explaining to the audience the procedure, I'm removing the casing and when that is done I can see what the problem is with this nice lady's air conditioner. The inside of the condenser is so plugged up that it looks like someone put a blanket across the inside. I plug it in and the compressor is on locked rotor. This means a $400 bill to repair this unit. Now I'm not angry any more. I just feel sad for this lady who, just a few minutes ago, I could have crosschecked with my hockey stick. I told her—and the rest of my audience—that she should have taken the air conditioner to the car wash, aimed a high-pressure water hose at the coils, front and back, and for five minutes of effort, she could have saved herself all of this aggravation and expense.

(By the way, this lady left in tears, apologizing for being so mean and emotional. It turns out she needed the air conditioner repaired for her 87-year-old invalid mother. I keep her air conditioner in my shop to show people how and why it is so important to keep the condenser clean.)

That lady had to dispose of her unit—the cost of repairing it was more than it was worth. But make sure that you have a good evaluation of any used room air conditioner before you dispose of it. Many have very little—if anything—wrong with them that some attention won't clear up.

What to Do with a Dripping Air Conditioner:
Some air conditioners drain water out of the back; others throw the water through the rear condenser. If you notice an older air conditioner dripping water, hold back on the temptation to drill a hole in the back underside of the unit. That is *definitely* the wrong thing to do-you will run the risk of drilling a hole in the refrigeration tubing and causing serious damage.

Don't Forget to Oil the Motor:
When your air conditioner was new, it came with a tag that suggested, "Oil once a year." Do pay attention to the advice—it

could save you $200, the cost of a new motor. Unfortunately, in the case of portable air conditioning units, the advice is easier said than done. Manufacturers haven't made it easy to get to the oil ports that lead to the motor. You will have to remove the casings, then remove the little plastic plug on the oil ports. Drop in about 20 drops of turbine oil (available at appliance parts stores), replace the plug and the casing and you'll sleep better.

Some Things to Consider:

• Don't operate your air conditioning unit when the outside temperature is below 65 degrees.

• Your condenser for both central air conditioning units is located outside. It should be kept free of debris—leaves, twigs, grass clippings, etc, and should be cleaned periodically using a high-pressure nozzle on your garden hose.

• Before hot weather really hits, set the thermostat for cooling, making sure that the temperature setting is high enough so that the air conditioner doesn't come on. I do not want to run the unit until a low-wattage heater built into the bottom of the compressor outside has been given a few hours to heat the oil in the bottom of the compressor. Only then will I turn down the thermostat to a temperature which will allow the unit to operate.

• After the air conditioner has been on for a half-hour, I then perform a simple test to tell me if the freon level is OK. I place a good probe-type thermometer into one of the registers. If the temperature registers at 20 degrees cooler than the outside temperature, I know that everything is working fine for this year.

Dehumidifiers

In the mid-1960s, when I started working for an appliance repair business, my boss told me that the easy money in repairs could come from consumers who inquired about fixing the dehumidifier in their basement.

"Tell them to bring the product to our shop, blow it out with the compressor and charge them $2 for air," he said. At the time, I couldn't figure out how this could equate to easy money because I was doing the job for next to nothing. His explanation made so much sense—even to my nimble little brain.

My boss added, "Every one of these customers will appreciate what you have just done for them. Who do you think they'll call when they need something repaired in their homes? Just like algebra, something equals something else."

It's been a long, long time, folks, since I've seen this kind of thinking in the service industry, but doesn't it make us all think about how good many of the old ways were?

Today we see thousands of dehumidifiers—many of them still good working units—dumped into America's landfills. The financial waste is incalculable. Yet few people know how to bring their dehumidifier back to life.

There are Three Things That Can Go Wrong with These Units:

• The coil on the unit fills up with frost.

• Frost forms on the coil.

• Or, there is no moisture dripping off the coil because it is coated in frost.

Funny stuff aside, the correction to the problem is even easier than trying to figure out what the problem is.

One of my good friends made the same mistake many Americans make. He called the other day to tell me that his dehumidifier had been frosting up while operating in his basement. He threw it in the trash and bought another one for $200. And now the new one was doing the same thing.

I told him that the months of June and July had been below the normal summer temperatures in the area, which meant that temperatures in most basements were lower than 65 degrees. At what temperature will a dehumidifier stop sweating water? You guessed it: 65 degrees. *When it is cooler than 65 degrees, you get frost.*

The Solution?

• Install the dehumidifier a few feet away from the wall, so it has plenty of air circulation.

• Make sure that the machine is on a level surface.

• If you have a drain in the floor, hook up a drain hose directly to it.

• Keep the windows closed in the area.

• When summer season ends, take the dehumidifier to the car wash, hose it, front, back and sides (but not the controls) then let it dry *thoroughly* for a few days before you plug it in or put it away for the winter. These units get so dirty inside that air can't move through them. When the compressor gets too hot to run, there is no way they can perform their function.

There are also times when the fan motor will lock up due to too much heat. Many people can change that motor themselves. Unplug the unit. Take the screws off that hold the casing on. Then change motors.

Remember to Oil the Motor:

When you buy both a new air conditioner or a new dehumidifier, the manufacturer will place a little tag on the fan motors which reads "Oil once a year." These manufacturers know how important it is to oil the motor fan and yet they give the owner little help in doing it.

The oil ports are located at the ends of the motor casing. The only way to access the ports is to disassemble the outer casings. It takes the Appliance Doctor just a few minutes to take the casing off a room air conditioner or humidifier, so you can do it in that amount of time as well. And remember, by faithfully oiling the motor, you are making sure that you won't have to spend $100 to replace the motor in your dehumidifier.

Once you have removed the casings, you will find that the oil ports have a little plastic plug which you will remove. Drop in about 20 drops of turbine oil (which is available at just about any appliance parts store). Replace the plug and the casing and you should have a smoothly running appliance.

Clean Your Units Faithfully

For more than 30 years, I've been taking room air conditioners and dehumidifiers to the local car wash. I don't even take the casing off; I just point the hose and aim the high-pressure water at all areas of the coils, on both ends of the machine.

I have told thousands of people to perform this maintenance every few years and I know for a fact that their units have operated well for many years. What I can't understand is the logic of a few people who will argue with what I've been doing so successfully. They tell me I'm wrong—but think about it: remember what a dehumidifier does. When operating, it is soaked with water and if it isn't, it's not working properly.

Let me tell you why you should take it to the car wash. Your room air conditioner and dehumidifier can become plugged up with dirt on the inside, dirt that you can't see from the outside. The drain channels for the water to exit the unit will become plugged up as well—which is why an ordinary garden hose will not do the cleaning job properly when you try to clean it at home. A dirty unit won't operate properly. A humidifier plugged with dirt on the inside will burn out the compressor and result in many hundreds of dollars of repairs.

Things to Remember When You Take Air Conditioners or Dehumidifiers to the Car Wash:

• Do not direct the flow of water at the control panel.

• Direct the water to the coils on the front and back and to any openings on the sides.

• Make sure that the entire unit is absolutely dry before you plug the machine in.

• If anybody questions why you are washing a machine and not your car at the car wash, tell them the Appliance Doctor sent you.

Hot Water Heaters

Folks, there isn't a lot of good news within the category of hot water heaters, but there is a lot of news—and a lot happening that you should be aware of.

Some time ago, I noticed that my dishwasher wasn't washing the dishes worth prunes. There was hardly any water in the bottom of the machine. I removed the water valve, thinking that I probably would have to change it. Instead, the screen was plugged with little white chips. I checked the screen on the washing machine water valve and found the same condition. This allowed for only a trickle of hot water to enter the machine.

I know that many homeowners who experience this same problem go shopping for a new dishwasher rather than calling for service or trying to fix the problem themselves. Many others bought new faucets, thinking that would solve the problem. What actually caused the cluster of white chips was a defective dip tube in their hot water heaters—and it is a problem that could affect as many as 24 *million* hot water heaters sold between August 1993 and October 1996. A class action suit has made the five manufacturers of these heaters are responsible for fixing the problem.

Six of our nation's major water heater manufacturers have admitted that there is a potential problem that could resulting in a loss of hot water pressure and temperature. The companies involved include American Water Heater Company, A.O. Smith Corporation, Bradford White Corporation, Lochinvar Corporation, Rheem Manufacturing Company and State Industries, Inc. Their units were built with plastic tubes (called dip tubes) to bring cold water into the heaters. These tubes are deteriorating prematurely and causing a loss in hot water supply. In compliance with a lawsuit settlement, consumers who have or have had loss of hot water or temperature can get their dip tubes replaced at no cost, receive reimbursement for related damages, and have related repairs made at no expense to themselves. What are the symptoms of a dip tube problem? A decrease in your hot water supply.

Call 1-800-329-0561 or log onto the Internet at www.diptubesettlement.com for details.

∽

Another class action suit was filed against State Industries, Inc., one of the six manufacturers mentioned above, because the manufacturer built hot water tanks without installing an anode rod and because State Industries used a plastic liner instead of glass. Electric elements have been failing prematurely and corrosion is eating the inner walls, causing leaks.

These water heaters were often sold under the "Duron" trade name, but other retailers have sold them under other names, among them, ironically, "Reliance." If the model number of a State Industries electric water heater is CD, SD, TCL, TD or PEX, it is a Duron electric water heater. Model numbers T6 SS8 and SSX may also be Durons. These tanks were installed on or after October 1, 1994 and in new homes purchased on or after the same date. A signed proof of claim must be mailed by December 31, 2001.

Benefits under the proposed settlement include a certificate for $20 towards the purchase of a new State Industries water heater, $15 for each failed heating element, up to $50 for the labor costs to replace each failed heating element, up to $150 to cover the cost of a new tank and as much as $150 for the labor to replace each failed tank. The company will also compensate for any damage done to their homes by leaking Duron electric water heaters, subject to the statutes of limitations.

Is there no end to the damage being done to manufacturers of hot water tanks by their very own stupid mistakes?

Care and Maintenance:
Every time a repair is made to your hot water tank, make sure that the plumber flushes out the tank to remove any residue. Otherwise, you will have problems long after the repairman

leaves your home. A thorough flushing will rid the tank of all residues—including all those little white particles.

Gas Lines

Recently, newspapers have reported that the gas line used 10 or more years ago to hook up stoves or clothes dryers might be dangerous to your health. The articles were based on information obtained from the Consumers Product Safety Commission in Washington.

According to the newspaper accounts, the commission learned of 200 cases where the old-style corrugated metal gas lines have sprung leaks. This has resulted in 35 deaths and 59 injuries. This type of flexible connector has not been sold for the past 10 years, but there are millions of stoves and dryers still operating after 10 years, and I'm sure that there are many still connected with this product.

It is a tragedy that the Consumers Product Safety Commission had to wait until 35 people died before they released information that might have saved those lives. Realize, too, that as these connectors get older and older, the likelihood of a leak increases tremendously. I am suggesting that the CPSC contact every major utility company across the land and put a warning notice on every utility bill.

It is my recommendation that you hook up a gas stove or gas dryer using *only* solid copper tubing with flared fittings. Use enough tubing so that you have several loops coiled at the rear—that will enable you to move the dryer for service and cleaning. These materials are all available at your local hardware store, where you can have the fittings flared. The hardware store industry is well versed on what has to be done to properly hook up your clothes dryer.

The CPSC reports that older corrugated metal tubes were used in hooking up ranges, ovens and clothes dryers. These uncoated brass flexible metal lines have fittings on each end that are soldered into place. The solder can fail—and that will result in a gas leak. Also, if the appliance is moved at all, it might cause the connector to break and leak gas.

I recommend that if you are using this type of 10-year-old connector, you shut off the gas to the product, remove the hazardous line immediately and replace it.

How to Keep Your Kitchen Appliances Cookin'

Stoves and Ovens

A little boy named Larry was two years old, with black, curly hair and a face worthy of a Beautiful Baby contest. His mother was baking pies for Christmas, using her new electric range, as he scampered around the kitchen. She opened the oven door, removed the pans she had stored there and then turned to reach for her pie. In a split second, the baby had spotted a bright red object at the bottom of the oven. Curious and thinking it might be a new toy, he reached for it and screamed in pain.

I was only ten years old, upstairs and doing homework when this happened, but I remember the terror in my mother's face and my brother's screams of pain.

I thought of this story as I was reading an article pointing out that every year more than 37,000 children under the age of 14 are treated for burns by hot liquids, hot food and hot tap water. In addition, every year 107,900 American homes have fires caused by cooking equipment. What happened to my brother gets repeated somewhere every day. That bothers me to no end.

I recommend that you install a door switch similar to the light switch on a refrigerator and when the door is open all the way, the alarm goes off. That could prevent a lot of house fires from occurring and prevent a lot of injuries. We could all make a difference if we safeguarded our kitchen and passed this recommendation on to a friend.

As Part of Your Holiday Preparations, Troubleshoot:

One of the stories most often repeated throughout the years goes something like this:

I had the whole family coming over and I spent all week preparing and all morning getting things ready. At around noon, I set the turkey in the oven and took a little nap. When I woke up, I opened the oven to check on the turkey's progress and I could barely feel any heat there—and there was no progress on baking the bird. I went into a state of panic. No matter which knob I turned, I couldn't get the oven any warmer. That's when I had to call the neighbors—whose oven was stuffed with their own turkey and stuffing.

Finally, in desperation, I drove halfway across town to a friend's house. We ended up eating our turkey dinner a day late.

The next day, a service technician turned a little knob around the clock and charged me $40. My stove has a keep-warm or hold feature and somehow while I cleaned the timer area, I touched the knob and didn't realize it. Did I ever learn a lesson the hard way!

This scenario and near-tragedy could have been prevented with a little forethought.

Many people don't use their oven section very often—which means that it should be checked in advance of an important meal. Here's how:

• Purchase an oven thermometer from your grocery store and place it on an oven shelf. Set the oven on 350 degrees, let the oven heat up for several minutes, and then check the temperature. A variance of 25 degrees is reasonable, even in new ovens. You can always increase or decrease that setting difference by turning the knob up or down to compensate.

• If you need service, call immediately. The service industry becomes exceptionally busy just before the holidays.

~

As a young man, I would watch my father make a primitive stove in the sandy beach in front of our summer home. He would dig a hole three feet by three feet in the sand and build a fire inside this hole. Before long, the sand would begin to boil and he would place a large cast-iron pot filled with navy pea beans and chicken legs into the sand pit. This secret family recipe would sit in the hole for hours while my father continually kept the fire going on top. He did this many, many times using the principle of boiling sand. My family still fondly remembers the great taste of the food prepared using this prehistoric method. Let me explain how we are still using sand today and how it can create an explosion.

When the burners and elements are made for your stove, there is a small, thin wire encased in sand that runs through the burner and element. Electricity heats the wire, the sand begins to boil, and the part becomes red-hot. When this works well, it heats the burner that heats your pot. But, if food spills and it is not cleaned off, its acidity will pit the burner or element, much like rust forming on the chrome bumper of a car. Eventually, the pitting action will eat through the burner or element until it gets to the boiling sand. At that time, atmospheric air comes in contact with the boiling sand and an explosion takes place that isn't loud, but terrifying to behold. Sparks can fly. So can hot, molten pieces of metal. Anyone within range will suffer from serious burns.

Many of the owner's manuals that come with new ranges fail to inform us to use a cleaning product with an acid base to clean our ovens. When you clean with this, cover your elements with tinfoil to prevent the acid from affecting the wire. Then remove the tinfoil. A product that I think is particularly effective in cleaning stove elements is Bon Ami.

Here's How to Properly Maintain and Check the Burners:

• Check each burner by setting the various controls to low, medium or high (if electric). Make sure that they operate properly on each setting.

• Check to see whether the burner ends are corroded. If the ends are not shiny and free of pit marks, they should be replaced—and the burner block along with them.

• Thoroughly clean burners and stovetops. The majority of top burner problems are related to dirty conditions. Spillover foods can cause pitting, which could eventually lead to an explosion of the part.

• Gas ranges no longer have pilot flames. They have ignitors, which are fragile and can break if the oven door is closed too hard. So many times I hear from consumers who have moved the range to lay new flooring or paint the walls and then discover that the burners fail to ignite. If you see the ignitor glowing bright red, do not assume the oven safety valve is the defective part. In 99 percent of the cases, it is the ignitor.

• Make sure that the appliance has been grounded properly, with proper voltage.

Other Important Safety Tips:

• If you have a gas range, make sure you crack a kitchen window when you use it, even in the coldest days of winter. Gas ranges introduce a small amount of carbon monoxide into the kitchen and cause headaches.

• If you have asthma, you may want to consider using only electric stoves. Research has noted that the nitrogen dioxide that is a byproduct of natural gas combustion can function as an irritant to asthma sufferers and may trigger asthma attacks. It is doubly important for these people to keep a kitchen window cracked whenever a gas appliance is used.

• Clean, shiny drip pans on an electric range can save you $25 each year in energy consumption. If you wrap them in foil in a mistaken effort to keep them clean, the foil can cause problems. It slows and partially prevents the heat from being conducted to the pots and pans.

• Use cooking ware with the flattest surface. Take a ruler and place it across the bottom of your pot to check for warping or curves in the surface.

• Always use a burner that is the right size for the pot.

• Self-cleaning ovens can reach temperatures of 800 or 900 degrees. This high heat is required to burn off the spilled sauces that ruin the appearance of the oven. Many times if a strong burning odor emerges towards the end of the cleaning cycle, it is coming from the cabinets next to the range, or from plastic tablecloths, plates or tableware within the nearby cupboards. Check your kitchen carefully and make changes in what you store near the stove.

~

Mrs. Gadsby of Southfield wrote to me to say that the clock on her 10-year-old electric range had stopped working and asked, "Short of buying a new clock, which I found out is $120, can it be repaired?"

In the old days, the television repairman had a product in his toolbox called contact cleaner. If your picture was fuzzy, you called the repairman, he came in and sprayed your tuner, and the picture looked great again. That same product is now available to consumers, who can find it at any hardware store. Many people have put their stove clocks back in working order by spraying the gears on the back of the timer assembly.

To do this, make sure you pull the cord or kill the power to the stove. By spraying the gears and turning the timer knobs at the same time, you may very well save yourself $120.

Microwave Ovens

I believe that it's important for you to know and understand how your microwave works and how it accomplishes such fast cooking. In fact, it will not only help you cook better, it may actually save your life or the life of someone you love.

Cooking in a microwave is really not so different from the old-fashioned frying pan method. When the food is heated, the molecules are spun into motion, rubbing against each other, producing heat, which produces a cooked product. In a microwave, there is a magnetron tube, which emits a wave into the oven cavity that is absorbed by the food.

Years ago, someone discovered that this wave moves the molecules at ten times the speed of conventional cooking. Many people have asked whether this wave remains in the food and, if so, whether it is harmful. What happens is that the wave is actually turned into energy when it enters the food. It does its job much the way a light bulb does its job.

Microwave cookbooks will tell you that it's important to let food stand for awhile once they come out of the oven. This is because the food cooked by microwaves has molecules still moving like crazy, even after the oven turns off. This is especially true of larger items. Foods may appear to be perfectly done when you shut off the microwave, only to become over-cooked by the time you serve your guests. How many of us have seen turkeys disintegrate or baked potatoes turn to dust?

Now, every microwave user should remember that you can't use metal inside your microwave. That is because the magnetron tube which sends the heating wave also receives waves. Metal objects in the microwave will reflect back up the channel to the magnetron tube and damage it. You will add years to the life of your microwave if you remember that whatever goes into the oven should absorb the wave, not reflect it.

Before you shop for a microwave, decide what you'll use it for. The size of the foods you cook will determine the size of the oven you will need. The wattage output determines the speed at which the oven cooks. Your budget will determine how much you want to spend—microwaves sell for less than $100 and more than $300.

Important Tips to Keep in Mind When Using a Microwave:

• Locate your microwave on a separate circuit, where there is plenty of room for good air circulation all around. Do not place cookbooks, knickknacks or anything else on top of it. Leave room for air movement behind it.

• Keep the inside of the oven free from food splatters and crumbs. Cooked repeatedly, they will form a hardened spot which acts like metal—and can be equally disastrous to the magnetron tube.

• Use a toothbrush to keep the door seal area clean of debris.

• Gently clean the ceiling area.

• Boiling a dish of water within the microwave oven will emit steam and make it much easier to clean the interior.

• Cure odor problems by boiling two cups of tomato juice and letting the juice stand in the oven for two hours.

• Never use an abrasive soap or material to clean the interior.

• Never slam the door.

• Push the touch pad controls gently—the gentler, the longer they will last.

To Repair or Not to Repair?

Repairs by the homeowner can either be money saving or death—causing, depending on your commonsense. I have many times on my radio and television programs told consumers that they could change the fuse (which they can buy from a hardware store for $5) in their microwaves. These fuses look like the old-fashioned car fuse and they are in a little holder that is visible once you figure out how to remove the casing to get to it. HOWEVER, ask a servicer about how to remove the casing before you attempt it.

AND...If you touch anything inside that microwave while it is plugged in, you may fry yourself to the kitchen floor—literally. (It's been known to happen!) Proceed with extreme caution.

If you don't know what you're doing, DON'T DO IT! An average of four Americans die every year while trying to fix their own microwave ovens.

Remember: *Whenever you work on electrical appliances, unplug them!*

Dishwashers

Not so long ago, dishwashing offered homemakers the chance to collect their thoughts and watch the kids play outside their kitchen window. Or, when she washed and he dried, it offered a couple the chance for a few quiet moments of conversation. Sometimes I wonder whether technology has made things better...or just different.

Restaurants are required to operate their dishwashers with boiling water to prevent food poisoning and other illnesses. Why should we be any less particular in our own homes? Have you ever wondered whether an ailment might be the result of improper dish washing?

In our house, I am in charge of the dishwasher and I feel pretty darn good about this responsibility. I'm not the boss in many ways, but I am the boss of the dishes. Here are some regulations that I've established in our house:

• DON'T try to save a few dollars by lowering the temperature of the water servicing your dishwasher. Your health is more important than the chance to save a few dollars—this is another case of penny wise, pound-foolish. The hot water tank should be set all the way to "high" or the highest temperature possible. If you have small children, use some caution here. There are gadgets at the hardware store that allow you to regulate water temperature in different locations. Dishwashers should operate at 140 degrees to be most effective. Test the water temperature using a candy thermometer.

• I always turn on the hot water faucet at the sink before I turn on the dishwasher. I allow the water to run until it comes out as hot as possible. Without doing this, you will never have the proper water temperature inside the dishwasher, the detergent will be unable to dissolve properly and the cleaning process will be ineffective. When this procedure is not followed, the impellers attached to the motor become covered with undissolved detergent, which will prevent them from spraying strongly enough to clean the dishes.

• I use Cascade detergent in a powdered form. Never a liquid.

• I always rinse my dishes because the dishwasher was never meant to be a garbage disposal system. Nevermind what you hear in the sales department.

• Once every six months I run a full jar of Tang breakfast drink (powdered) through a wash cycle to clean out the machine. (See the 'Tang Treat Recipe' below.)

• I always let my dishwasher go through the entire dry cycle using the heat cycle.

• I use the exact amount of detergent recommended for the machine. We have a water softener, so that means no more than two teaspoons. City water in homes requires 8 teaspoons. The rule of thumb is to use one teaspoon of detergent for every grain of hardness in the water.

The Tang Treat Recipe:

• Turn on the hot water at the kitchen faucet and let it run until the water is at its maximum temperature.

• Turn on the dishwasher until it has filled with water and you hear the arms swishing—it usually takes about four minutes.

• Shut off the dishwasher and open the door.

• Empty the entire container of Tang powdered breakfast drink directly into the water at the bottom of the dishwasher.

• Close the door and start the dishwasher again. Let it run through the entire cycle. (Make sure that you don't drop the small silicone package within the Tang jar into the water.)

• Sit back and rest assured that you are giving your dishwasher a treat that will serve you well, too.

∼

General Electric has recalled 3.1 million dishwashers produced between April 1983 and January 1989 because they were built with a slide switch that can heat up, melt, than ignite a fire. The U.S. Consumer Product Safety Commission has reported more than 50 fires that have occurred because of this defect.

Actually, what GE is doing is not a recall. Should you be able to prove that you purchased a new GE dishwasher during that time frame, GE will offer you a rebate check for $25 if you want to buy a new dishwasher of another brand or a rebate ranging from $75 to $125, depending on what model of new GE dishwasher you choose. The new dishwashers, by the way, cost between $399 and $499.

The defective models under the General Electric and Hotpoint names were manufactured with model numbers GSD500D, GSD500G, GSD540, HDA467, HDA477 and HDA487.

Let me point out what GE is actually doing for you, their valued customer: If you're lucky, they are covering the installation costs of a new machine.

What about all those people who own apartment complexes and must replace dozens, or even hundreds, of dishwashers at once? And what about the impact on our environment when 3.1 million dishwashers are suddenly dumped in landfills?

After I ran my first column about the so-called recall, New York State Attorney General Eliot Spitzer sued General Electric, alleging that it offered a sweeter deal to businesses that owned

GE dishwashers. They were offered inexpensive repair kits and instructions for replacing the switches.

What's going on here? Listen to this statement because every one of you has heard it before: "GE, America's most admired company, has been bringing good things to life for more than a century." It's certainly true in this case—but the good things happening are happening for GE. They are now in the position to sell millions of new dishwashers, all at once to individuals. I've talked to appliance dealers who tell me that they have five people in at a time replacing their recalled machines.

Why won't GE just fix this defect on their product? It is a simple switch which I would estimate would cost no more than $5 to buy and $15 to repair. It takes 10 minutes to change the switch and ensure that the consumer has a dishwasher capable of running reliably for another few years. What is being perpetrated on 3.1 million GE customers is simply not fair.

Interestingly, just prior to the recall announcement, GE announced that the switch in question would no longer be manufactured. Coincidental? I don't think so.

I've said it before and I'll say it again: It's a crying shame what business in this country gets away with.

Refrigerators

When I was a young boy, somewhere around the age of 13, and living in northern Ontario, high-tension power lines were installed that cut a swath 100 yards wide through the wilderness. Down these man-made trails my friends and I would pedal our bikes, loaded with sleeping bags and fishing poles, until we came to a small creek loaded with fish.

On one of these expeditions, after pumping our legs for three miles or so, we came across an old deserted gravel pit, where we found a brand new shiny car called a Thunderbird. Slumped inside the vehicle was a gentleman who had decided to end it all with a game of Russian roulette. It was not a pretty sight—in fact, it haunted me for years. And what has never left me is the memory of the odor that emanated from the body, which had sat there for several weeks.

In my work in the appliance industry, I have many times been forced to remember that foul smell because it has revisited me often.

In 1971, when I was a customer relations manager for the Amana Refrigeration Company, I had to travel to Port Huron to investigate a compressor failure for a six-month-old Amana freezer. I walked into the house of a couple who had just returned from a three-month vacation. During that time, their large upright freezer, loaded with game and fish, had failed. The stench was horrible. It had permeated the walls of their home and even the living room curtains.

Many times I have smelled the same stench while on service calls. Every week, I receive several calls from consumers who ask how to remove the smell from their product. Some homeowners think that it comes from Freon—which it doesn't. They overlook something that has spoiled in the back of the crisper drawers.

If you ever have this problem with lingering odor, let me suggest that you wash the product using pure tomato juice. When you're done washing and rinsing, go to the hardware store and purchase a bottle of Smells Be Gone. If this still doesn't work, take the product outside and let the sun shine on it for several hours. The hotter and brighter the sun, the better.

Remember: By taking care of your appliance and by paying attention to its contents, you can save yourself a lot of work, agony and expense.

~

Many people have asked me how long they should expect a refrigerator to last. I tell them what I'm telling you: The answer can be long and confusing. Because the Freon (a brand name) used in refrigerators and freezers to cool the units is destroying the ozone layer and creating this big hole which just keeps getting bigger and bigger, the federal government has enacted new regulations about its use and reuse. Because Freon is so new, we really don't know how long a new refrigerator should be expected to last. It could be five years, ten or even twenty years, but I strongly suspect that it will be fewer rather than more.

The secret to adding years of life to a product and cutting back on energy consumption is as simple as ABC. Keep it clean where it counts. The condenser must be kept free of dust, lint, animal hair and other debris. The condenser is the bunch of black tubing that is sometimes located on the back of the product, but more often underneath it.

When the condenser is clogged, the compressor becomes so hot that I could fry an egg on top of it. When that happens, the wattage draw is so high that it sometimes blows a fuse. The fan motor and defrost timer are hurting from all the excessive heat load. The life of the product is being slowly drained from it because of that dirty condenser. Cleaning the condenser will save you from having costly repairs, save on the cost of running the appliance, and save the appliance for more years of use.

Here's how to clean that condenser. Every three months *pull the plug* on the refrigerator and pull the refrigerator away from the wall. Take the lower cardboard cover off of the backside. Use a brush with a long handle to shake loose all the dirt you see on the condenser, then vacuum the debris. Replace the cardboard back. Then, remove the front toe plate and do the same there. Use care around the fan motor blades—don't bend them. Clean the blades tenderly with a toothbrush. By doing this regularly, your energy bill will stay where it should be rather than increasing as much as $10 per month. The refrigerator's operational noise level will no longer sound like a runaway train. And your appliance will do a better job of food preservation.

The average life expectancy of major appliances today is much less than products built more than ten years ago, so it is in our best interest to do what we can to prolong its life expectancy. In my years of experience in the appliance industry, I have seen products that I would classify as pure junk compared to what the same companies built in the yesteryear.

Long ago, during the Kennedy administration, a Consumer Bill of Rights was passed. It's too bad that manufacturers can't remember its contents.

~

During the hot summer months, refrigerators and freezers have to work overtime to keep their contents cold. In fact, the industry generally estimates that refrigerator repairs increase three-fold during the summer. Condenser fan motors will be the most common component to fail, causing a typical service invoice to exceed more than $125. On top of that, thousands of dollars in food loss will occur and thousands of consumers will feel compelled to buy new refrigerators.

Fact: Many of these problems would not happen if the home-owners would clean the condenser underneath the refrigerator.

Fact: A new condenser costs $500. So, it is worth the time to keep it running smoothly.

Why do compressors fail at much greater rates in the summer months? Because the refrigerator is overworking.

There are also some do-it-yourself repairs for refrigerators that can save you money. Please keep in mind, however, that appliances have electricity flowing through them and it is *not* meant to flow through you. *Pull the plug before you begin any repairs.*

One of the most common service calls on a refrigerator is related to the defrost system. You can compare the defrost timer to a clock that fails to advance and put the refrigerator in the defrost mode.

There is a heater inside the freezer compartment which is attached to the freezer coils. The defrost timer, which is constantly turning, gets to a certain point and then it stops the refrigerator from running completely for 30 minutes. During this time, the timer is sending power to the heater, which will then melt the snow accumulation on the freezer coils. Picture a small amount of frost on each finger and blow air through all your fingers. This is how a fan motor circulates cold air throughout the complete refrigerator and freezer.

Should the defrost timer stop running, the heater never comes on and the snow begins to accumulate, to the point where the fan cannot blow any air between the coils. The fan motor can no longer pull cold air from the freezer coils and the first place that you will notice this will be in the refrigerator section. Temperatures will soar to 50 and 60 degrees.

The most common cure for this problem is to change the defrost timer. But wait. Test it first.

Now, the hardest thing to find within the refrigerator might be the defrost timer. The size of the palm of your hand, it is connected to four wires and mounted to a plate with two screws.

The plate has a hole the size of a dime so that you can manually turn the knob. You can call the manufacturer and ask where the defrost timer is located on your model. When you find it, turn it clockwise slowly until the refrigerator stops running.

You know then that you have put the refrigerator into the defrost mode and that the refrigerator should start to run again in 30 minutes. If it stays in defrost any longer than 30 minutes, I would suggest that the timer needs changing.

A good indicator of a defrost problem is not only the warming in the refrigerator section, but also snow inside the freezer section. Another indicator is a drain pan that is filled with water following the test you have just performed.

Remember that you need to pull the plug on the refrigerator while you are changing the defrost timer. The timer itself should cost you about $35 and you cannot return it for a refund if your prognosis of the problem is incorrect.

Be sure. Be safe. Be assured that you can do this.

~

I recently received a call from a man who had hauled his refrigerator up north and hooked it up only to discover that it didn't cool. It had worked fine when he had left the area.

I told him what I'm telling you now: Remember that any time you carry any kind of refrigeration product—such as a refrigerator, dehumidifier, freezer or air conditioner—you must always let it stand in its normal position for at least two hours before you plug it in. That's to make sure that all of the compressor oil migrates back down to the bottom of the compressor. You can run up a pretty expensive repair bill if you don't follow that piece of advice.

I wonder why appliance manufacturers don't pass on that simple piece of advice?

∿

A few years ago a friend of mine moved here from Boston and asked me if I could get him a good used refrigerator that he could install in his laundry room as a back-up refrigerator for entertaining. I had a 1945 model that we used in the store to keep pop in and I decided to sell him this at the 1945 price.

Last week we were chatting and my friend asked, "Why can't I get the same cold in my five-year-old refrigerator?" I wish that the appliance industry could answer that question.

Progress is not always in a forward direction. Our grandmothers' first refrigerator was capable of keeping food at 33 degrees. The average new refrigerator on the market today maintains a temperature of 40 degrees or warmer. Folks, I am the Appliance Doctor and the coldest I can get my own three-year-old refrigerator is 38 degrees in some sections and 42 degrees in another. I've tried every possible setting on the thermostats and that's the best that I can do.

It stands to reason that a refrigerator that can keep foods colder can preserve foods longer. I think that it's a crying shame that my grandmother's refrigerator could keep milk colder than my current refrigerator (which registers 43 degrees—10 degrees warmer than her old one).

We have to keep that in mind that with the warmer temperatures, food must be disposed of more quickly. The U.S. Department of Health states that the average American suffers the signs and symptoms of food poisoning (stomach cramps, nausea, diarrhea) no less than six times a year. Most of us think that we have a case of the flu or something else going around, but in reality, we may be responsible for our own problems by keeping food too long in the refrigerator. I have a rule in my house that says, "Any perishable item will stay in the refrigerator no longer than three days. On the fourth day, it is in the trash."

∾

I don't know about you, but in my years in the appliance service industry, I've learned a lot about the noises—good and bad—that appliances make. We notice those noises especially in the winter, when all the windows are closed and the volume goes up on appliance hums, hisses and whirrs. Let me try to explain what to expect when your refrigerator is not working properly.

Refrigerator hums and hisses usually come from fan motors that circulate air throughout the product. Sometimes they occur when you close a door and trap too much air inside—some of that air has to get out and it will find its own way of doing so.

A gurgling noise comes from the refrigerator boiling within the sealed system of tubing which runs throughout the product. Clicking and snapping noises are common; they may come from the defrost timer activating the defrost heater. The defrost system usually works at long intervals, such as six, eight or twelve-hour periods. During defrost, you may also hear water slowly running into the defrost pan. The violent sound of a defective bearing in a fan motor will bring your senses to full awareness—this is *not* associated with normal running.

Water dispensers and ice makers will give you noises like buzzing, thumping, trickling and even the clatter of ice falling into the bin. A rattling can occur when a drain pan under the refrigerator has been placed improperly.

High-energy compressors use less energy, but run a lot more than you may be accustomed to. Keeping the condenser clean under the refrigerator is most important—not only for noise levels, but also for a machine's long life and reduced energy costs.

Energy-saving Tips for Freezers and Refrigerators:

• Make sure that your refrigerator and freezer doors are sealed airtight. Test them by placing a lighted flashlight inside the refrigerator or freezer during the night hours with all the lights off in the room. Stand on a stool to check the top of the door. Use a purse mirror to check the bottom of the door for signs of light. Take a hair dryer and heat the area of leakage on the seal itself. Stretch the seal outward; it has a tendency to come back to its original shape. If it's torn, coat the area with rubber glue and let it dry overnight. This tip has saved thousands of people from spending hundreds of dollars.

• Clean the door gaskets (the flexible strips around the door that seal the cold air in) with a sponge or soft cloth soaked thoroughly in a mild detergent and warm water. Rinse and dry. NEVER use cleaning waxes, bleaches, strong detergents or petroleum-based cleaners on gaskets.

• Locate your freezer and refrigerator away from heat-producing equipment, such as the range. Also, they should be out of direct sunlight.

• Assure proper ventilation. Maintain adequate clearance from the walls and cabinets—see manufacturer's recommendations.

• Keep condenser coils clean. If dust or dirt is allowed to accumulate, it will impair the appliance's operation. Every four months use a vacuum cleaner and a refrigerator condenser brush to clean out dust. (A long-handled brush is best.)

• Open the door as little as possible. Make a mental list of the many things you need before you open the door, then take them all out at once, quickly.

• Build a counter space or shelf next to the appliance so you have a handy place to put the items from the refrigerator.

• Try to put things in the same spot so you can easily locate them and reduce the amount of time the door is open.

• Label all foods clearly and legibly. This eliminates confusion and permits quick removal of the food. Place more frequently used food items in front.

• Store produce loosely in your refrigerator to allow good air circulation.

• Keep containers from blocking air vents in your refrigerator.

• Cover all bowls that have liquid in them. This will keep the interior humidity level lower and reduce the work of the compressor.

• Cool very hot foods for a short time at room temperatures before placing them in the refrigerator—but don't let them stand for too long. Bacterial growth will result if foods are left unrefrigerated for too long.

• Close the door gently. Don't slam it. You lose less cold air that way.

• When going on vacation, use up your perishable food and empty the refrigerator completely. Unplug it. Prop the door open and put baking soda on the shelves to avoid mildew.

• Keep your freezer full and closely packed together for more efficient operation.

• Wrap food properly to help prevent excess frost formation on sides and coils in your freezer. Thaw meats before broiling.

• Set food from the freezer into the refrigerator for one or two days before you plan to cook them.

• Select the right size refrigerator for your family and your shopping habits.

• Defrost the freezer when one-quarter inch of frost has accumulated (on a manual-defrost model). The frost build-ups cause the cooling system to work harder.

• Raise the front of your refrigerator and freezer one-half inch higher than the rear. This will help the door close more easily and provide a better seal.

Freezers

I recommend a manual defrost freezer, even though it can be a pain in the ankle to defrost. The reason is that a self-defrost freezers have a heater which brings hot heat directly in contact with your frozen food several times each week. That heat can cause frozen foods to be affected in taste and in nutrient depreciation. With a self-defrost model, you have a fan pushing cold air throughout the inside. (That's another reason why you have to take extra care in how you wrap your food.)

I want the food I cook to be as fresh and wholesome as possible, so the most important tip that I can give on the manual defrost freezers is always make sure that you do not use anything sharp or metal when you defrost it. If you poke a hole in one of the freezer's aluminum shelves or tubing, you might as well kiss it goodbye. Super Glue won't help.

⁓

The W.C. Wood Company has recalled 345,775 chest freezers sold between January 1991 and February 1996. They have a defective lock mechanism that can be opened without a key, so it is possible for a child to climb inside and have the door close—and they will be unable to open them.

These freezers were sold in sizes of 7, 10, 12, 15 and 22 cubic feet. All were white or almond in color and they carry the names Woods Brand, Quickfrez, Danby, Crosley, Whirlpool, Roper and Estate.

If you know the location of one of these chest freezers, please call 1-800-227-6874. The Wood Company will send you a modification kit to repair the problem. If you have one of these freezers, unlock the lid and place the key in a location that cannot be reached by children.

Ice Makers

The icemaker in a refrigerator is what I call an accessory item that corresponds to electric windows in a car. You can crank windows by hand or touch a button; you can fill plastic trays with water and empty them or you can have a machine do it for you. Both upgrades will cost more and may add repair bills into your budget when you least expect them.

I'll be blunt. Typically, ice maker's average five to seven years of life span—which is, hopefully, less than the life span of your refrigerator. I believe in spending $4 for some plastic ice cube trays rather than the money manufacturers charge to include an automatic icemaker with a refrigerator. But, I'll admit that I'm in a minority, so I'll be more helpful.

Many readers have called to complain that their icemakers produce cubes that taste terrible. The cubes might also contain tiny unidentified floating objects. Or the icemakers may have broken down entirely. This is a synopsis of possible problems:

• The floating objects in ice cubes can often be attributed to something as simple as the flaking of paint in the mold of the ice maker, which can be corrected with the installation of a new ice maker.

• Foul-tasting water from the dispenser often can be corrected with the installation of an in-line filter on the copper tubing that supplies water to the rear of your refrigerator. If you spend the extra money to do that, keep in mind that you need to purchase a new filter every six months or so, or the water will taste worse than not having a filter at all.

• When the unit refuses to produce any ice at all, the problem is usually the ice maker valve. You can remove the valve (see below) and take it to a reputable appliance service company for testing before you purchase a new one. Unfortunately, these valves are basically the same ones that have been manufactured for the last 25 years. I've not seen the needed improvements to prevent flooding caused by the failure of this part.

The future holds higher prices for consumers when it comes to replacing and repairing appliances, so the more you can do yourself towards maintenance and repair, the better off you will be.

The water valve is the most common cause of problems in icemakers. Let's try to fix it ourselves and save some cost.

If you pull the refrigerator away from the wall—do this gently, watching that you don't damage the kitchen floor—you will see a piece of copper tubing leading from the inlet water valve to the refrigerator. (Note: This tubing should always be copper, not plastic, because it's always under pressure.) This valve is a very easy part to remove.

First, *unplug the refrigerator*. Next, follow the tubing until you come to the shutoff valve, and shut the water off before you go any further. Place some heavy-duty towels underneath, just in case of leakage when you begin taking things apart. Then return to the water valve and, with a little crescent wrench, disconnect the water line. Also disconnect the lines that lead the water supply to the inside of the refrigerator and freezer. Draw a little schematic picture to remind yourself what and where these wires connect, then pull the electrical connections off the coils on the water valve.

Remove the screws that mount the water valve to the base of the refrigerator, and the next thing you know, the complete water valve is in your hands.

Take the valve to your favorite appliance repair shop and they can check it for you by hooking it up to water and electricity. Water valves can cost as much as $60 for original equipment, less for non-OEM parts.

The water valve can interfere with more than ice making. It can allow water to trickle into the icemaker, which will cause the cubes to stick together or a big glob of ice to form in the bucket. This is because particles of dirt in the water jam the seals inside the water valve.

Don't take the valve apart and try to repair it. Buy a new one.

Coffee Makers

While doing the radio show some time ago, I got a call from a woman who asked if I knew anything about automatic coffee makers, the kind that sit on the kitchen counters of most American households.

Her problem was related to a switch that turned the machine off and on, and the question brought to mind a conversation that I had with firefighters, who told me that drip-type coffee makers are responsible for starting many kitchen fires.

The safest way to use this product is to make sure that you always unplug the cord when the machine is not in use. Most homemakers keep the machine plugged in all the time and this can cause the ON/OFF switch to overheat and even cause a fire.

This is one of the simplest of repair jobs; unplug the coffee maker after you have used it.

Water Softeners

Last summer, I decided to go on my first-ever diet, and the particular diet that I chose insisted that I drink plenty of water. After drinking water straight out of the tap, I decided that I couldn't stand the taste of chlorine. So I spent $40 on bottled water, although I'm always a little suspicious of where bottled water comes from. That investment disappeared faster than the money I spent to buy it.

Finally, in an effort to save money, I decided to spend $3,000 for a water softening system and a water purifier.

Installing the equipment would take Mr. Jake three hours to do, I was told. And then, I would be able to enjoy the purest water I'd experienced in years.

The first thing that Jake had to do was shut down the house water supply by shutting off the valve just above the main water main in the house.

The valve, which is 27 years old, had probably never been moved and it sure wasn't going to move on this day. It was frozen solid, so Jake decided to shut off the valve just below the meter. That was OK with me. He managed to shut it off until it was almost completely closed. Then it broke.

The flow of water into the house is now at the rate of two gallons per hour, which means that it takes forever for toilet tanks to fill. That also means that Jake can't install any plumbing while water is flowing through the lines.

I called the city water department and they scheduled a man to come out at nine the next morning. I called a plumber as well, so that he could install a new valve as soon as the city shut off the water at the street. Meanwhile, we had company staying with us. I hooked up a garden hose to my neighbor's outside faucet to fill the toilet tanks whenever necessary.

The next morning, the city guy shows up and so does the plumber. The city guy has a metal detector to find the cap on the water shutoff at the street. But he can't find it. He calls another city inspector. He can't find it either.

After three hours of digging enough holes in my front yard to look like gopher city, the city foreman shows up and decides to shut off the water in the entire neighborhood. That means that we must inform the neighbors first.

Meanwhile, I'm being kept pretty busy filling toilet tanks and jugs of water, plus watering $300 worth of new landscaping that has just arrived.

In the middle of the afternoon, the city foreman shows up again and starts probing into a three-foot hole dug earlier. He finds the shutoff valve. I could have kissed him.

By the time I pay the plumber, who stood around for four hours and who will have to change every valve and faucet in my house, I have spent a lot of money and have learned a big lesson.

Please, make sure that every shutoff valve in your house is working like it should be working.

Garbage Disposers

A few months ago, I took Valorie and our daughter Hollie out to a restaurant noted for its ribs and special sauce. The next day, we enjoyed a light dinner consisting of leftover ribs and it was my turn to clean up the kitchen.

Both Val and Hollie were sitting at the kitchen table when I put the bones from the ribs into the garbage disposer and turned it on. You should have seen their faces as pieces of bone flew around the kitchen. Some even hit the ceiling. Worse still, I had managed to plug both sides of the sink, as well as the complete drain line which leaves the kitchen.

I knew from experience that unclogging that blinking drain line is no fun. For the next hour, I became a plumber.

Whatever happened to the good old days? I used to have a Maytag disposer in which you could put a handful of nails and they would come out as dust. I once took a whole turkey carcass and broke it up and ground it up in my Maytag. I certainly could have used one on that day.

～

The cost of a disposer ranges from $39 to $239 today and without a doubt, you get what you pay for. In fact, if you are house-hunting and want to know how quality-oriented the builder is, simply open the kitchen sink cupboard and write down the model number of the disposer, then check its price. A good-quality model that will perform adequately will cost $150 or more.

What happens with less expensive models is quite simple. If they can't chew the garbage into very fine pieces, then you will plug up the drain line from the sink to wherever it goes—as I have learned several times, the hard way. If you have a drain line from the sink that leads straight down, that will help prevent blockage. However, most homes have lines that lead away from the sink at different angles; that makes a high-quality disposer imperative if you really want your garbage disposed of.

Most of us pay little to no attention to this appliance. There is virtually no maintenance involved. However, one consideration is the possible bacterial growth within the product. We've all experienced the smell that comes from the sink when we forget to grind something up for several days.

Think of your disposer as an extra large coffee can with a motor and cutter wheel at the bottom. The disposer's walls are lined with food products that are not always washed clean away when the machine is turned on.

Tips for Keeping Your Disposer in Top-notch Condition:

• I make it a habit in my house to fill the disposer with ice cubes once a week, let them sit for an hour, then turn on the disposer. That cleans it and sharpens the blades.

• Make sure that the machine never runs for more than one minute at a time.

• Running the cold water is a must to keep the cutters cool and prevent the motor from overheating.

• Letting the water run into the sink for 30 seconds or so after you shut off the disposer is a good habit. This flushes food particles through the smaller drain lines under the sink.

• Many service problems are caused by the twist-ties used for bread or the little probes that come with meat products. It doesn't take much to jam the disposer, particularly the cheaper ones. You can use a pair of needle-nose pliers to clear any obstacles that have jammed the unit—but shut it off first.

• Many disposers have reset buttons on the underside of the unit; these pop out when the disposer jams and refuses to run. After you have cleared the obstacle, make sure the reset button is pushed in before turning the unit on again.

• *Safety alert:* Mounted in the bottom of the disposer is a little relay which can provide a spark when you turn it on. Many homeowners store plastic trash bags under the sink adjacent to the disposer. When you turn on the disposer, the spark could ignite what is in storage. Check for a potential fire hazard.

The Ins and Outs of the Laundry Room

Washers

I well remember my mother, bless her soul, doing the washing back home in northern Canada. She had a big aluminum tub that she would fill with hot water that had been boiling on the pot-bellied stove. My father's underwear and my baby brother's diapers would all be placed in this tub to soak for a few hours before she washed them in the wringer washer.

She would send me downstairs to remove the clothes from the tub and put them into the wringer machine, and she would always tell me not to spill any of the Ajax on the floor or on myself. I can still remember the smell of that Ajax when I would fill a large cup full.

I think I grew up wearing the cleanest and whitest long underwear in the world, but I hated those drawers because that rough material itched. The second thing that bothered me was the trap door in the posterior. (You young folks reading this have no idea what I'm talking about, do you? I was warm, but you are lucky!)

Recent headlines have warned about how washing

machines can spread bacteria and the story is very alarming to me, but it also reminds me of how clean my mother was. Believe it or not, she would even use a toothbrush to clean the corners of our old oak kitchen floor.

But back to washing machines and bacteria...

According to a study conducted by Charles Gerba, an environmental microbiologist at the University of Arizona, household washing machines may be transferring bacteria from one item to others in the tub during a typical wash cycle. More than 60 percent of the machines that he studied tested positive for coliform bacteria, an indicator of *fecal contamination*. Further tests confirmed the presence of a germ called staphylococcus, which comes primarily from underwear.

Gerba did further tests and concluded that bacteria such as E. coli, salmonella and mycobacterium fortuitium placed on one cloth would indeed spread to all other articles of clothing sharing that wash tub.

As if this isn't alarming enough, he found that these germs remained in the clothes even after putting the washer through a second wash cycle. When he was all done, he found that the tub inside the washer was contaminated with these germs.

Running the clothes through a clothes dryer cycle for 43 minutes killed some of the bacteria—but not all. Dryer heat eliminated the E. coli, but the others were still present.

Gerba recommends that consumers launder their underwear last, and that bleach is used. He discovered that bleach kills 99.99 percent of all bacteria.

Now I understand why my mother insisted that I wear clean long johns every day. A half century before this research, she had standards we all should envy.

There are so many things to be aware of in this world that

it can make your head spin. I, for one, select those that I'll remember and pay particular attention to. After finding out about bacteria in washers, I told Valorie that from now on, I'd do the whites portion of the wash.

That's right, folks. I'm going to soak all shorts, underpants and white footwear in a laundry tub with hot water and bleach. After that, I will run them through the washer and dryer.

(For all you curious people, by the way, I no longer wear long johns.)

~

One of the mysteries of the modern world haunts many folks. Just what is it that causes snags on certain articles of clothing while they are being washed? This question has led me to a series of investigations.

The story begins with a question from one of the news reporters at the radio station. She asked why she had ruined so many sweaters in her four-year-old washing machine. The problem of snags, she said, didn't happen in every load, just occasionally.

I told her that in an effort to correct the situation, I have taken a pair of panty hose and rubbed them on the surface of the inner drum to see if there was a rough spot. To no avail. I have replaced the agitator. That didn't help. I have removed the inner drum to see if there was anything stuck between the tubs. I never found a thing.

In an effort to arrive at the elusive answer, I studied her washer. It turned out to be a European model that I didn't even recognize, one which had cost a whopping $2,000. Obviously this was a universal problem that knew no geographic boundaries. I was stumped. So, I called the manufacturer.

A man with a heavy accent immediately asked if the lady in question was large-breasted. I answered in the affirmative, to the best of my limited knowledge. I'm not in the habit of looking past a lady's eyes. The speaker then accused her brassieres of being the culprits. He explained that the under-wire that helps add support will occasionally come out of the undergarment and lodge itself between the two tubs. In fact, it won't even have to come out of the garment; it can poke out of a tiny hole in the garment and do the damage. He added that this piece of metal wire will cause all kinds of snagging problems.

When I reported back to the reporter, she investigated and found that that was indeed the problem. I thanked her on behalf of all my readership.

~

Many homeowners suffer from a washing machine that walks all over the laundry room floor. The solution is easy to prescribe, but it can be difficult for many to perform. They need to shore up the wooden floor where the machine sits, so that it can sit level.

When will homebuilders realize that a washing machine must sit on a cement floor to operate properly? Any other floor will cause problems with vibration.

~

Colleen Milligan of Birmingham followed my recent suggestion to level her Speed Queen commercial heavy-duty washer in order to get rid of a crackling noise during the agitation cycles, but called again to say that it still makes noises. She noticed that if she tilts the basket slightly, the noise disappears until it re-centers itself. She asked how to get inside of the machine to see if anything was loose.

The washer's problem may be a pump belt that has stretched and flaps together when it is running. This is something easily diagnosed.

To remove the front of the machine, remove two screws at the bottom of the front panel, pull the front off and everything is exposed. If you, too, have this problem, check the tub springs as well.

~

Do you know that you need to winterize your washing machine?

If you live in an area that sees frost and snow every winter, you need to slow down the cold water coming into your washer during the winter months.

In the winter, the cold water line that hooks up to your city water has a tremendous pressure drop. The cold water feeding your washer will be colder than during the summer and that is why you need to gently adjust the faucet handle behind the washing machine.

You do this by lifting the lid and filling a cup full of water while making the adjustment. Using a candy thermometer, play with it until you have 100-degree water when you set the machine for "warm wash."

Rinse water has always been a topic of conversation among the experts. Although some disagree with me, I believe that cold water rinses remove soap and stains better than warm or hot water rinses. End of discussion. Sometimes I think manufacturers just add all those buttons on the front of the washer console to make it looking appealing.

~

A note about recalls: General Electric has found that some transmissions in their GE, Hotpoint, RCA and Profile washers manufactured in the U.S.A. between January 1993 and June 1994 are susceptible to failure. Under GE's standard limited warranty, a consumer will be expected to pay approximately $200 for a transmission replacement. If you own one of these products and you experienced a transmission failure, your product will be repaired at a special reduced rate. Contact GE at 1-800-432-2737.

Clothes Dryers

It was many years into the 1900s before man created a mate for the washing machine. For more than half a century, the majority of American housewives hung clothes out to dry, winter or summer. In those days, doing laundry was an all-day ordeal. Women or helpful kids carted baskets of wet clothes from the warmth of the house into the heat of a blistering summer day or the frigid chill of a winter's day and one by one, the articles of clothing and household items were hung up to dry.

I remember my mother filling a clothesline 30 feet long with her weekly wash. And every time, I'd see my despised long johns dancing in the wind. But I also think about the times when she would make me smell the fresh-aired sheets as she made the bed. The odor of bed linen dried by hanging out in fresh, clean air has a fragrance that the world may never know again. My mother used to say, "This is how heaven smells."

Some of the Hamilton clothes dryers made in the 1940s and '50s are still operating, believe it or not. The old adage is true: They *don't* make them the way they used to.

The clothes dryers of today have many more features, are more energy efficient, and they dry with a much lower temperature than yesteryear's models. An older dryer may be very hard on your clothes because of the high temperatures it relied upon and because the garments of today, like the machines of today, arc not made the way they used to be.

Today's dryers need to be cared for to make them last. The movement of air through the dryer to the outside is of the utmost importance to a long-lasting dryer. The vent line should be solid aluminum—*do not use a plastic vent line.*

The folds and crevices of plastic lines and the warmth of the air flowing through them attract birds and small animals. A restriction to the air movement that travels through your dryer to the outside will cause a lint build-up inside the dryer, which can easily be ignited. Commonsense says that the old-fashioned solid aluminum vent line has no ridges, is smooth, and will let the air, plus the lint, go to the outside much faster.

Believe me, folks. Seventy percent of service calls for dryers are related to vent lines. Plastic vent lines are responsible for countless fires. Fortunately, the new state construction code requires metal vent lines for the dryer.

To prevent animals from invading your dryer line, clean the flapper area with a tooth brush and spray the surface of the outside flapper with an insect repellent used for ants and bees. DO NOT put a nylon sock or screen over the vent exit. This will cause a restriction of air and create a lint build-up inside the vent line.

The lint filter should be washed with soap and water every month and the dryer taken apart and vacuumed out every two years. The size or weight of the load you place into your dryer will determine how long it will last or how quickly you will have to replace parts.

Watch what you put in a dryer. A cloth soaked in cooking oil can ignite into a fire. So can containers of combustible materials stored above or near a dryer.

Do not close the laundry room door when you use your dryer. The dryer uses 200 cubic feet of air per minute while it is operating, so you need to supply it with constant fresh air for good-smelling clothes.

When and if your dryer starts to make squeaks or rumbling sounds, stop it immediately and call a repairman. Those sounds are signs that something is definitely going wrong. You will not only do more damage to the machine if you continue to run it, you will also run the risk of a fire.

~

Every week I speak with someone who has just had a gas clothes dryer delivered, only to discover that the appliance store deliveryman refuses to hook it up. And the homeowner can't figure out how to do it because the copper tubing that hooks up to the back of the dryer won't fit into the pipe sticking out of the back.

With the purchase of a $3 elbow and a little advice, you can solve this problem yourself. (In fact, if the deliveryman is carting your old dryer away, remove the elbow from that machine and use it on your new one.)

Simply hook the elbow to the two connectors, and you're in business.

~

And, speaking of repairs, you might as well know how to change the belt on your dryer, as well. It's easy enough to do if you have a Whirlpool or Sears (Kenmore) dryer that is at least two years old—going as far back as a model manufactured in the 1970s.

Open the dryer door and look inside. You'll see the drum that spins the clothes. Around that drum is a long one-piece belt that turns the drum like a chain turns a bicycle wheel. When you had to change the chain on your bicycle, you had to remove the rear wheel from its forks to get the chain around the rear sprocket. In dryers, the only thing preventing you from putting the new belt around the drum is the front of the dryer. Let's go to it.

First, *unplug the machine.*

See the lint filter on the top right-hand side? Remove it. Do you see the two screws in the opening where the lint filter slides in? Remove them.

Take a medium-size flat screwdriver and gently slide it under the top front edge, three inches from each side. The complete top of the dryer will pop up in front and you can put a broom in place to prop it up so that both of your hands are free.

Take one of your hands and remove the power cord from the outlet, if you haven't already done so, so you can complete this job without killing yourself.

All gas dryers and some electric models have a kick panel that goes across the bottom of the machine. Take your screwdriver and insert it along the topside of this panel. Pop it off.

Now, get down on your knees. Look at the bottom of the front panel, which is still on the dryer, and on each side you will see a 5/16 nut bolt. DO NOT remove these bolts. Simply

LOOSEN THEM, using a 5/16 nut driver or ratchet wrench.

While you are down on the floor, lay down so that both arms and hands are free. Place a flashlight with the beam pointing at the motor on the right side of the cavity. You will notice an S-shaped bracket which clips into two slots on the floor of the dryer. This is called an idler pulley and when you purchase a new belt, there will be instructions on the back of the package that describe how the belt goes on and how the belt loops through this idler pulley. READ THEM.

Stand up. You now know how a service technician feels after doing this for 20 years.

To remove the front panel, check once more to make sure you have pulled the electric cord out of the outlet. Take out the two 5/16 screws you will see in each top corner. These are facing from inside to the outside on the top panel.

Once you remove these screws, the front panel will fall off, so hold your hip against it. If you look, you will see two or three wires going to a door switch. You must remove these wires before you take off the front panel. Make yourself a little drawing of where the wires connect, then remove them.

Folks, you have just taken your Whirlpool or Kenmore dryer apart and now you can vacuum out the inside and change your dryer belt. Use extreme care when cleaning, so that you don't break the igniter, which is located at the end of the gas valve assembly.

Congratulations on a job well done and on your savings! Wasn't this easy?

～

Several years ago, an attorney called me and asked if I could be retained as an expert witness in a case regarding a domestic fire caused by a clothes dryer. The plaintiffs had lost their entire house due to that fire and the insurance company was refusing to pay them a cent because they considered it a case of arson.

This was not the first case that I'd been asked to become involved in. I inspected the burned-out hulk of the dryer and it was immediately apparent that the clothes within the drum ignited. I wasn't sure of the reason. The insurance company, manufacturer's service representative and the engineer hired by the company maintained that the clothes within the dryer caught on fire because they might have been doused with a solvent.

You see, folks, neither they nor I knew the cause of the fire, but they sure weren't going to blame it on their product. They chose to blame the poor unfortunate family who had already suffered the loss of their entire home. In America this year there will be 14,000 house fires that are directly related to the clothes dryer in the laundry room. I wonder how many other home-owners have been—or will be—given a rough ride by the insurance industry?

Let me give you some facts about this particular make of dryer. I was very familiar with it. I knew from first-hand experience at least a dozen owners of this make of dryer who had been fortunate enough to put out fires in their dryer before it ignited the entire house. Something was seriously wrong with this product, I told the U.S. Product Safety Commission, when members came to me to investigate. "The clothes are igniting inside the dryer drum because the drum fails to turn and at the same time the gas valve assembly becomes ignited. With the flame hitting the bottom of the drum, anything will ignite. "Without a doubt," I told the commissioners.

Several years later, I was sent a copy of a memo circulated only to employees within that dryer manufacturing company seven years before the fire that I testified about. The memo states that the motor switch can fail on certain dryers and cause the gas valve to operate while the dryer drum does not turn. But the U.S.P.S.C. is taking its sweet time investigating.

∾

Speaking of fires, other dryer fires can be directly attributed to the lint in a dryer's lint trap, vent line and bottom of the dryer. In more than one case that I know of, the dryer continued to run, despite the blockage and the dryer blower had forced the flame up the back wall of the laundry room. Within two minutes, the entire laundry room was engulfed in flames. This was in the middle of winter, so the airtight condition of the home meant that the fire was starved for air and it forged ahead on its destructive path.

This is only one of many tragic stories that I have heard while investigating plastic or flexible dryer vent lines. I write, I preach, I talk about the grave dangers involved in using one of those lines. Don't use plastic or flexible dryer vent hoses! Spend the few dollars to save your house—and perhaps even the lives of your family members.

∾

Several years ago, newspapers and talk shows were touting the idea of a product that allows recycled dryer air back into the home during the winter months, to serve as an additional heat source. Let me tell you, folks, I don't believe that this product should be sold in this country.

When the load of clothes is removed from the washing

machine, it still contains some additives from the laundry detergent, particularly if the washing machine isn't spinning as well as it should. When you place the clothes in the dryer, not only are they drying, but they are also shaking off these byproducts, by virtue of the tumbling.

The most serious of the byproducts is chlorine and it is very dangerous to breathe. Chlorine that is airborne can cause copper solder joints to leak and can even cause a hole to eat through the heat exchanger in your furnace. It can do many other, more harmful things, but in particular, think of what damage chlorine can do to your lungs. You don't want to jeopardize your health. Take care. Send the hot air from the dryer outside, where it belongs.

~

Speaking of dryers and your health, along comes a lady named Martha Stewart, who talks well, hosts a TV show, loves to garden and cook, produces a monthly magazine, and is listened to by millions of Americans. I liked what she was saying until she wrote a column about the laundry room and how installing cupboards above the washer and dryer was a great idea for using space that is otherwise wasted. She even suggested what products you could store there—most of which were, by the way, flammable.

Don't take that advice!

I have spent years telling consumers that it is wise to keep the areas around your clothes dryer clear of everything. Do not place items on top of the dryer or behind it.

Every year, as I've mentioned before, 14,000 American homes will suffer from fires caused by clothes dryers—and possibly three times as many are not reported.

When the fire occurs, it is usually underneath or in the back of the dryer. The flame has a natural path, going up the wall, and if you have shelves with flammable materials within it, you have just added fuel to the fire.

The clothes dryer in your laundry room is a metal box where your clothes spin in very hot temperatures. The burner creates one-third of the amount of heat produced by a furnace, yet it doesn't have a steel heat exchanger. The burner flame lies exposed behind a sheet-metal casing and a lot of lint can accumulate around it.

I don't trust a bear in the woods and I feel the same way about my dryer.

I think that I'll send a copy of this book to Martha Stewart.

~

When you're visiting someone's house, take a look at the dryer. See if it sticks out away from the wall. In many cases, you'll see the dryer protruding six inches or more into the room.

That wasted space is the result of having to install a solid metal elbow at the vent exit on the dryer. Well, I'm delighted to say that this problem could be history, thanks to a hardworking guy named Dennis Gomulinksi, who, for 20 years, has delivered and installed appliances. He has invented a device he calls the EZ Vent System to vent a clothes dryer, which is easy to install and allows the dryer to sit flush against the wall. Best of all, this system does not restrict air movement from the dryer.

For more information, call EZ Vent Systems at 1-810-469-0600.

~

Pat Brown of Farmington wrote to say that when her clothes come out of the eight-year-old gas dryer, they smell "worse than a skunk." Her husband was insisting that they buy a new dryer and she asked my opinion.

I told her what I'd tell you: This problem is such a simple thing that it will amaze you. The American home is sealed so tightly from outside air that the Environmental Protection Agency says that indoor air may be more hazardous to our health than outside air. When using your dryer, open a window to introduce fresh air into your house. This is particularly true if you are painting or varnishing or using cleaning solvents.

The other day another lady called me with the same problem. After a little question-and-answer, we determined that her problem resulted from a new caulking job around a new window, which gave off a strong odor. Any time your gas dryer is operating, it needs air for combustion, just like your furnace does. It will draw air from all areas of the house, not just the laundry room. This air goes through the burner assembly and then into the drum. The wet clothes retain the odor and you won't get rid of it until you wash them again.

You just saved yourself a service call or the price of a new dryer, Mrs. Brown.

~

Watch out for things that go thump or screech, when the sounds are coming from your dryer. These are indications of something quite serious going on with your machine.

Screeches and thumps indicate that the drum rollers, which

support the drum, may be worn out. This is the cause of many fires in this country. If a dryer starts to make unusual sounds, pay attention and act quickly. The quicker the repairman comes, the less expensive the call should be.

∿

Some new dryers are being manufactured with cheap cloth-type lint filters. I wonder how many millions of replacement filters consumers will have to buy every year now.

The filter may be the most common part sold in the United States. The metal lint filters used by some manufacturers have far greater durability. The operating manuals that come with dryers emphasize the importance of cleaning the filter and keeping the lint screen free of lint. You should strip it of lint every time the machine is used and clean it with warm water and a toothbrush monthly. The better the air movement that you have through the screen, the quicker your clothes will dry and the cheaper your electric (or gas) bill will be.

∿

In another section of this book, I cover the topic of how to deal with dryers that have survived floods, but the issue is important enough to discuss in two sections.

Contrary to what consumers are told, the gas valves on dryers, like the gas valves on water heaters and furnaces, are not sealed units. There is one area on a dryer where moisture can enter—the hole where the gas exits the valve.

The inner portion of the valve is sometimes made of rubber diaphragms, which seal the gas changers. These diaphragms *must not* come in contact with anything that will corrode them. Sewerage backups can corrode these diaphragms and there is no way that the homeowner will become aware of this before it's too late.

Here's the truth: If your dryer is ever involved in a flood, don't take any chances. We all know that a wet motor must be allowed to dry completely or it will die the minute you turn it on. The same goes for the gas valve. Replace it as soon as the floodwaters have receded.

When the gas valve is not replaced, consumers report gas coming out of their dryers months after the flood—even when the dryers were not in use. Recently, a university study revealed that diseases can be spread through clothing that is washed in machines containing accumulated fecal matter. In fact, service technicians in many localities now wear rubber gloves when fixing a washing machine. Baby diapers are concerns, as well. These health issues are being studied like never before.

I know. I know. You homeowners who have suffered from sewer or water backup have a lot on your plates already. But don't do half a job and leave your family susceptible to even greater problems. Do yourself a favor. Change the gas valve. It's not hard to do. Even if you have to pay someone to do it for you, do it.

∼

Safety Tips for Dryers:

• Make sure that you have a metal exhaust vent on your dryer—absolutely no plastic or flexible material.

• Clean the lint trap every time you use the machine. Lint is combustible and will ignite.

• Keep papers, clutter, dirt and dust away from your dryer.

• Crack a window when the machine is operating.

• Think again before installing shelves above the dryer. Fires generally start underneath or behind a dryer and a sudden fire will feed too quickly on shelves above the machine, particularly if they hold combustible materials.

• If your gas dryer has been in a room that has flooded, replace the gas valve immediately—don't take a chance.

• Make certain that you vent dryer air outside—don't use it as an additional heat source.

• Clean the vent flap routinely and spray it with insecticide to prevent little critters from moving into the warm climate for the winter.

Outside, Around and About the House

Smoke Detectors

One day, I stopped by an elementary school just when the fire drill was being conducted. I watched the kids file out of their classes in an orderly way and watched the teachers count heads to make certain that everyone was there.

The system has not changed since my elementary school days. It was apparent that the principal thought that they had not evacuated the school quickly enough. Watching her check her watch and talk to the teachers reminded me of the captain on the Navy ship on which I served. We competed against other ships in the North Atlantic squadron and our captain was never satisfied with our time. Only later did I find out that he had lost a ship during the war because of a fire.

If we stop and think about it, people in charge, especially people in charge of little ones, should be well prepared, in advance, to know what they need to do in case of fires. They should be trained by experts to react and do what is necessary.

As homeowners, we should be just as educated. When was the last time you conducted a fire drill in your house? That goes for all of us, senior citizens, singles and couples, as well as the parents of small children.

What have you done around the house lately to prepare for a fire or carbon monoxide leak from that old furnace (the one that hasn't been checked in years)?

There are a million house fires in the United States every year. What have you done to prevent adding your house to that statistic? The horror stories of entire families wiped out because of carbon monoxide poisoning (which is odorless and colorless) or because of insufficient or inoperable smoke detectors goes on and on...

Let's stop tragedies from happening. Be prepared.

Lawn Tools

Five years ago, after living in a condominium for many years, Valorie and I moved into a house. With that came a new responsibility—lawn care. But I tackled the challenge with gusto. I told myself that I got my exercise in winter by playing hockey two nights a week, so, I'd get exercise the rest of the year by pushing a lawn mower.

I bought a used mower in good condition, had the blade sharpened, and bought another one, just in case. I know that a dull blade can ruin a good-looking lawn. Next, I removed the foam-type filter around the carburetor and cleaned it with dishwasher detergent and hot water. I used my brand new leaf blower to dry it. I installed a new spark plug and made sure the connector was tight fitting and wouldn't fall off from vibration. I sprayed all movable cables and linkages with a light oil.

Then...on to the exercise. I removed the four wheels, and tightened the bearings, making the wheels harder to turn, so I could really build up some sweat when I pushed that machine.

I'm sure the folks who walked by told each other, "Look at that old guy. He's so out of shape, he's going to drop dead cutting his grass!"

When the season is over, I run the mower until the fuel tank is empty. Old gas will produce a varnish-type coating that can cause engine and carburetor problems. I then do the most important thing you can do for a small engine: I changed the oil.

It is always best to change the oil before winter arrives. The old oil has contaminates in it that can cause damage to engine parts during the storage months. Change the oil after the machine has been used, when it is still warm. And make sure that you use the grade of oil recommended by the owner's manual. Most oil filling stations will dispose of the old oil for you.

As with any consumer product, if you care for your lawn tools, they will take care of you. A little maintenance on your yard helpers will allow you to enjoy your summer season with the least aggravation. In like manner, once winter is over, do the same thing for snowblowers, snow mobiles and fishing augers.

∼

In my extensive research for this topic, I traveled the distance to my garage and then to the garage of my good friend Gary Gray, who comes closer than any friend to the Tool Man mentality. He owns everything there is for yard care and tools. I spoke with him, then dropped in on our neighbors the Herrimans, who have the most beautiful back yard in the world. (In fact, whenever the opportunity arises, I tell people that their yard is my yard.) From these research excursions, I have compiled some things worth thinking about.

First of all, let's talk about a necessary accessory to outside work: the ladder.

Are you aware that it is against the law to deface a ladder? Indeed, it is. You cannot drill a hole or put a sticker onto a ladder. You cannot paint a ladder or do anything that may cause or hide a stress crack.

On to lawn tools. Weed wackers, trimmers, rototillers, hedge shears, edgers and leaf blowers work under extremely dirty conditions and to keep them in tip-top condition, you should clean them after you use them. I wash them down carefully using a garden hose, then use my leaf blower to dry them. Cleanliness is the best way to keep your tools operating well for many years.

Another way to keep power tools working well is to use the extension cords recommended in the tools' owner's manuals. Using two cords instead of one is often a sure way to destroy a product.

~

Snowblowers

A snowblower certainly saves a lot of back-breaking effort, but in order to make sure that your snowblower works when the snow is blowing, take a few moments for its care and maintenance before winter arrives. If your machine needs any work, early fall is the time to do it. Treat the snowblower like you would your car, with routine maintenance. Empty it of gas at the end of the season. Keep it clean.

Touchpads

Last winter, a woman called the show to tell us that she had fixed her treadmill touchpad control board simply by wiping a clean cloth dampened with warm white vinegar across the surface, then drying the area with a tissue. (Don't use a paper towel—it will scratch the surface). She learned the technique when I advised her to do that on her kitchen stove touch pad. It really works.

Strange, isn't it, how something so simple is never found in instruction books that come with appliances?

Grills

If you have an older outdoor barbecue grill that is rusty and you're wondering if it's worth repairing, you should use caution.

Annual statistics from the Consumer Product Safety Commission reveal that thousands of Americans will suffer from severe burns this year due to cooking outside. Some of those injuries will be due to the use of old, corroded equipment. The rest of it is just plain carelessness.

If you stop and think about the fuel source alone, that should be enough to catch your attention. The propane tank attached to your barbecue is close to the fire that sits above it. Things could get hot around there if you're not careful.

• The fittings that attach the hose must be checked and you must make sure that they don't leak. A cup of water mixed with a heavy concentration of liquid dishwasher detergent can be used for the bubble test. Take a little sponge and apply the solution to all the connections, and then look for bubbles. If you see them, then you know there is a leak.

• Take the grill apart and check the areas where the gas leaves the burner valves. This is the path the gas must take to ignite and travel to the burners. If these parts are falling apart due to rust, replace them. The Servall Company is a good source of replacement parts and so are many of the outlets that sell barbecue grills.

• Always have a fire extinguisher available near the barbecue. It is a good idea to have one in the kitchen, too.

Now, you should know some facts about the propane tank. Propane gas is lighter than aviation fuel and it has a quicker ignition point than the gas you put in your car. If a cigarette lighter can explode and create a flame 12 inches long and 4 inches wide for several seconds, imagine what an exploding propane tank can do. The next time you have it filled, ask the technician to check the valve for any leaks.

• Never store a full tank of propane gas in the trunk of your car on a hot summer day—or at any time of the year, when the sun can beat on the tank.

• As soon as you finish cooking, shut off the burners and the valve on top of the tank.

Take heart. You can always go back to the "primitive" grills that use charcoal briquettes and a lighter. You might find that when you experiment with different forms of wood chips on that grill that you like the flavor better!

(Remember, you can grill steaks briefly outdoors, wrap them well and put them into the freezer. Then, in the dead of winter, when the temperature is so cold you don't want to venture outdoors, you can finish cooking that steak in your microwave and marvel at how it tastes just like it came off the barbecue.)

Automobiles

Recently, I took my car to one of those fast oil-change places—the same shop I've been going to for the past five years—to have the obvious performed. A few weeks later, I raised the hood to check the windshield washer level and found the dipstick for the transmission oil lying on top of the engine. I figured, "New guys in the place. A mistake. No big deal."

A month later, Valorie asked me to take her new car on my fishing trip to Canada because she loves me. The new car had 3,000 miles on it, so I took it in for an oil change and check-up.

The new guy in the oil change place greeted me like a long-lost cousin and informed me that because this new vehicle took a total of eight quarts of oil, he was going to give me a deal. He would put in eight quarts and charge me for seven.

I said nothing, but smiled, and I'm sure he took that as approval to go on with the job. Within 30 seconds, I had the owner's manual opened to the page with all the specifications for this particular car. *The car takes six quarts of oil, not eight.*

I beckoned the technician over to my window and asked him sternly if he knew what he was doing. I asked if his book said the car took eight quarts. He replied that it did. I then showed him the owner's manual that said six quarts.

"Holy smokes!" he replied. "I'm glad you showed me that."

I've been asking myself over and over, "Was this an honest mistake?" I don't know of an American car that takes eight quarts of oil. When an engine gets too much oil, you get smoke and blown seals.

How many engines received eight quarts of oil from this business? Or was it a scam to give me six quarts and charge me for seven?

Something else to think about—and be aware of.

~

The other day, as I filled my gas tank, I noticed a teenager at the other pump, smoking while he filled his tank. When the gas was entering his tank, the cigarette was no more than two feet away from the point of entry.

My first thought was to stay cool.

"Do you know you shouldn't be smoking around a gas pump?" I asked.

His reply was polite and he dropped the cigarette to the ground and stepped on it with his tennis shoe. Thank goodness there wasn't a gas spillage on that spot.

That incident makes me wonder about the prevailing lack of common sense. When I spoke to the gas station manager about the incident, he gave me some eye-opening written information. Its reminders are definitely worth passing on.

• Portable gas containers can build up a static electric charge during transport. Consequently, when the container is not placed on the ground for filling, its static electricity could be discharged and result in a fire when the filling begins. Please place the containers on the ground during filling. Keep the nozzle in contact with the container. Never fill a container while it is inside a vehicle or its trunk, the bed of a pickup truck or the floor of a trailer.

• Remain at the vehicle's fueling point even when using the nozzle's hold-open latch. Don't re-enter your car. It could result in the your becoming charged with static electricity. Then, when you return to the fueling point, that static electricity could be discharged and you would catch on fire.

• Don't use cellular phones or other electronic devices while dispensing motor fuel.

• Should you see anyone else violating these common sense rules, inform the attendant. State law says that gas station attendants will then shut off the fuel supply to pumps where customers are committing an error.

Perhaps that—and these reminders—will save their lives. Let's hope so.

Grocery Scanners

Although we don't often take the time to acknowledge them, a store's scanners, particularly grocery scanners, are appliances that have a major impact on our lives. And unless we are informed consumers, we can almost count on losing money over a scanner.

Several years ago, Michigan Attorney General Frank Kelley revealed the results of his fourth annual scanner accuracy survey of Michigan's retail stores. Investigators bought a total of 280 items in various parts of the state. The scanners registered the wrong price on at least 14 percent of the items—20 percent in some parts of Michigan. Sixty percent of those prices were overcharges.

In response to his study, the attorney general warned the public that we have more to lose in routine shopping expeditions than we have to gain in a two-hour sale.

Telemarketing

Studies have shown that American companies rake in more than 100 billion dollars each year using unethical practices. Five years ago, the Federal Trade Commission published new rules regulating the telemarketing industry. These are worth reviewing:

• It is illegal for a telemarketer to call you if you have requested that you not be called.

• You cannot be called between 9 p.m. and 8 a.m. You must be informed up front if it is a sales call, in addition to the identity of the seller and the product being sold. If the call involves a prize, no payment or purchase of anything can be required as a condition of winning.

• It is illegal for a telemarketer to misrepresent any information about the product or service that the call concerns.

• You must be informed of the total cost of the goods or services being telemarketed and of any restrictions involving the purchase or use of that product or service. If the call concerns a prize promotion, you must be informed of the odds of winning.

• It is illegal for a marketer to withdraw money from your checking account without specific, verifiable permission.

• A telemarketer is not permitted to lie or use threats to get you to pay, regardless of the type of payment involved. You cannot be forced to pay for services ordered prior to actually receiving them.

Resources You Need
to Know About

Corporate Ownership

• AB Electrolux, a Swedish company, owns White/ Westinghouse, which manufactures the following name brands: White/Westinghouse, Coronado, Frigidaire, Gibson, Kelvinator, Sears' Kenmore Stacked Washer.

• General Electric makes Hot Point, General Electric and RCA appliances.

• Masco owns Thermidor/Waste King.

• Maytag owns Gaffers and Stattler and Jenn-Air and Norge, which makes Norge, Admiral, Crosley, Magic Chef and some Montgomery Ward appliances.

• Raytheon owns Speed Queen, Amana, Caloric, Glenwood, Modern Maid and Sunray.

• Tappan makes Tappan and some Montgomery Wards products.

• Whirlpool owns Whirlpool and Kitchen Aid.

Manufacturers

Sears' major appliances are manufactured by Whirlpool, General Electric and/or White/Westinghouse.

Whirlpool makes refrigerators, gas dryers, dishwashers, washers and dryers. Call 1-800-253-1301 with questions or complaints.

GE makes refrigerators, electric ranges and dishwashers. For questions and complaints to GE or Hotpoint, call 1-800-626-2000.

White/Westinghouse makes the Kenmore stacked washer. Call 1-800-245-0600 with questions or complaints.

Amana	1-800-843-0304
Athens	1-800-233-0498
Brown Stove Works	1-800-251-7224
Caloric/Modern Maid	1-800-843-0304
Carrier	1-800-CARRIER
Dacor	1-800-772-7748
Emmerson Quiet Kool	1-800-332-6658
Estate	1-800-253-1301
Fedders	1-800-332-6658
Frigidaire	1-800-451-7007
Gagneau	1-617-255-1766
General Electric & Hot Point	1-800-626-2000
Gibson	1-800-458-1445

Glenwood	1-800-759-1616
Insinkerator	1-800-558-5712
Jenn Air	1-800-688-1100
Kelvinator	1-800-323-7773
Kitchen Aid	1-800-422-1230
Maycor	1-800-688-1120
Maytag	1-800-688-9900
Meile	1-800-843-7231
O'Keefe & Merritt	1-800-537-5530
Peerless Premier	1-800-858-5844
Roper	1-800-447-6737
Sanyo	1-800-421-5013
Sharp	1-800-447-4700
Speed Queen	1-800-843-0304
Sub Zero	1-800-222-7820
Tappan	1-800-537-5530
Thermador	1-800-735-4328
Welbilt	1-516-365-5040
White/Westinghouse	1-800-245-0600
Whirlpool	1-800-253-1301